Golden Hands

Hamlyn House

Volume 17

Contents

Volumes 16 to 18 are a continuation of the previous books and extend and develop the techniques and designs already given for dressmaking, tailoring, knitting, crochet and embroidery.

There are chapters on how to create your own design details in dressmaking and on making up your own knitting and embroidery designs.

There is a new section on costume design including basic animal costumes—cats, tigers, rabbits—and twelfth and nineteenth century costume designs.

Also introduced in these volumes is a new look at special crafts—suede and leather crafts, hat making, enamelling, collage, bead weaving and batik are just a few of them.

These volumes begin again at page 1 but to avoid confusion the index numbers that relate to volumes 16 to 18 are printed in italic.

Published by
Marshall Cavendish Publications Ltd,
58 Old Compton Street, London W1V 5PA and
Hamlyn House Pty. Ltd, 176 South Creek Road,
Dee Why West, Sydney, Australia.
© Marshall Cavendish Ltd 1970, 1971, 1972
© Fratelli Fabbri Editori 1966, 1967

Printed and bound by Dainippon Tien Wah
Printing (Pte) Ltd, Singapore.

Crafts/preserving flowers

It doesn't matter whether you have a big garden or a small one, or even none at all, as long as you can get into the countryside there are masses of flowers, grasses, seed heads and leaves that can be picked and preserved for decorations.

A charming Victorian art revived, it is this easy accessibility of the basic materials which makes the craft so appealing.

Dried flowers have dozens of possibilities for decoration: preserved whole they make formal vase arrangements, table displays, wall plaques, and Christmas and party decorations. Pressed flat, they make charming collage pictures, table mats, book covers, book marks and greeting cards, to name but a few.

The choice of flowers

Gather flowers for preserving in the spring and summer, and for best results as soon as they have opened. If blossoms are too full blown, they are likely to either disintegrate or lose their colour. Flowers which will dry easily fall into two categories, the everlasting flowers such as Rodanthe and Acroclinium and others called 'soft flowers', some of which can be dried successfully if the process is quick. Here is a short list of flowers which can be preserved for whole flower decorations:

☐ Rodanthe: a small, deep red everlasting flower.
☐ Acroclinium: a rosy coloured annual everlasting flower.
☐ Statice sinuata: long stems of pink, mauve, violet, white and yellow.
☐ Statice limonium (sea lavender).
☐ Honesty: sometimes called 'silver pennies'.
☐ Chinese lanterns: orange lantern-like bracts.
☐ Cornflower: pink and blue.
☐ Love-in-the-mist: excellent for seed pods.
☐ Hydrangea: mature flower heads can be preserved.
☐ Delphiniums: blues, mauve and purple; small spikes preserve best, picked young.
☐ Golden rod: yellow gold spikes.
☐ Godetia: pink and red.
☐ Star of the Veldt: mixed colours.
☐ Marigolds: yellow and orange.
☐ Larkspur: pinks, mauve and purple.
☐ Sunflowers: double varieties of perennial types can be dried successfully.

Choosing for pressing

Almost any kind of flower can be gathered for pressing but it should be remembered that in pressing, bright colours will fade. Blues can fade to pale brown and bright red is likely to turn into chocolate

▲ *A standing arrangement of dried flowers, grasses, ferns and poppy seed heads*

that some of the stems should be pressed in a curve for variety. Here is a list of grasses suitable for preserving:

☐ Briza maxima: nodding heads—ideal for Christmas decoration when glittered.
☐ Lagurus ovatus: (hare's tail grass)—like a squirrel's furry tail.
☐ Stipa pennata: (feather grass).
☐ Timothy grass

Leaves

Many wooded stemmed leaves such as beech, pittosporum, lime and laurel can be preserved on the branch by using a glycerine solution. Beech leaves are popular for this kind of preserving because the range of colours which can be achieved is so beautiful. The earlier branches of beech are cut, the deeper the colour will be after preserving. Branches gathered later will turn a light tan colour. Elaeagnus, camellia, box and many evergreens are also well worth preserving using the glycerine treatment.

For pressing purposes, tree leaves should not be picked when they are green because they fade. The colours of autumn foliage are beautiful and will keep their colours without fading, and fallen leaves can be collected, even if they are damp. Include the leaves of plants such as clematis and those with grey and silver colours, such as cineraria, diamond, artemisia, and absinthium in your collection. Raspberry leaves are grey on the underside and so is the gazania leaf, and the addition of these leaves to a collection is recommended.

Seedheads and berries

Some seedheads, collected while they are still green and unripe, can be successfully preserved by the glycerine method. Experiment with different kinds of flowers and plants to find out the colours and effects. Many are prettier left until they are ripe, and are preserved by drying—poppies, spiraea, delphiniums, columbines, for instance, and, of course, honesty. Chinese lanterns are gathered when the lower lanterns are just beginning to colour.

Some vegetables produce attractive seedheads for flower arrangements—parsley, fennel, onions and leeks, for example, as do many wild flowers and shrubs. Look for plants such as knapweed, types of cow parsley, dock, ripple-wort and teasles. Berries can be preserved, but for only a few weeks, by brushing them with a thin glue soon after they are picked.

Methods of preserving

Drying flowers

Wherever possible, cut flowers with long

brown, so make allowances for these changes when a pressed flower collection is being built up. Experiment with different kinds of petals and flowers and note the colour changes as they dry. Beautiful collage pictures can be made in tones of beige, pale browns, grey and silver white. Yellow flowers are good for pressing—buttercups, for instance, retain their colours for about a year—but even if flower petals are inclined to turn to tones of brown, their colours, combined with silvery leaves and autumn leaves, will give a wonderful colour range with which to work. Ideally, flowers should be picked

in the middle of the day when they are dry—try to avoid picking when damp.

Grasses

Grasses should be picked before they are fully mature to prevent their shedding seeds. A collection of grasses can therefore be started quite early in the summer and a good variety should be gathered, including some of the less decorative kinds. In whole flower arrangement, grass stems can be used for mounting flower heads and leaves, their flexible stems falling into pleasing curves quite naturally. Grasses can be pressed too, remembering

▲ *Hanging ornament using sycamore, barley ears and wild grass*

▲ *Hanging ornament using larch cones, ash and brome grass*

▲ *Thank-you card using flowers, ferns and seed heads*
▼ *Bookmark using flowers and birch leaves*

▲ *Matchbox top using buttercups, grasses, rush and vetch*
▼ *Table mat with a bird motif using leaves and honesty pod*

▲ *Door finger plates using spring and summer flowers and mounted under glass*

such as a shed or outhouse. The darker the better because light will turn the grasses into hay.

Preserving leaves

Split branch stems upwards for about two inches and immerse them immediately in warm water. Leave the branches for a few hours and discard any on which the leaves curl. Make a solution of one part glycerine to two parts hot water and insert the stems. As the stems only require two or three inches of solution, use a narrow vessel—a tin can for instance—for the preserving fluid, and stand the tin in a bucket so that the branches are supported. The leaves will 'turn' in about three weeks.

Stems

As the stems of some dried flowers turn brittle, the stem can be strengthened by inserting a piece of fine wire through the centre of the flower, giving it a twist under the calyx. Alternatively, paint the stem just under the flower head with latex adhesive. This will dry stiff and clear and looks quite natural.

Natural looking false stems for flower heads and odd leaves are made with preserved grass stems—Timothy grass is particularly useful for supporting flower heads. Pierce the centre of the flower with a match stick and thread the grass through, stem first, until the grass head touches the flower centre. Trim the grass head off and pull it through a little more until it is almost invisible. Separate leaves can be attached to grass stems with a touch of latex adhesive.

Pressing flowers

Method 1. Pick the whole flower and place it as soon as possible between two sheets of blotting paper and then immediately between the pages of an old book which has absorbent paper pages. Several flowers can be arranged together on the sheets as long as they do not touch. When one sheet is complete, turn six or seven pages on in the book and proceed through until the book is full. Then place a heavy weight on the book—bricks or a flat iron will do, and leave it quite undisturbed for about four weeks. Do not look at the flowers at all while they are pressing. Leaving them quite undisturbed and the heavy weight on top is the secret of successful pressing.

Method 2. For flowers with a hard centre or a hard formation, use a flower press.

Presses are often inclined to spoil delicate flowers and the book and brick method is better for these types of flowers.

stems. Tie into small bunches and hang heads downwards in a cool shady place with air circulation. It is important that the place be dry because damp conditions will make the flowers go mouldy, and if there is too much light the colours will fade. Some flowers, such as helichrysums, lose their heads when the stems are dried out. These can be mounted on false stems. An alternative method of drying whole flowers involves the use of powdered borax or Silica gel. Flowers dried in borax dry in about three weeks—only three days are required for flowers buried in Silica gel.

Method. Cover the bottom of a box or biscuit tin with the powder and then either lay flowers face down or stand them on their faces, depending on their structure. Pour more powder all over and round them, lifting the petals now and then, so that the flower is surrounded by powder but still retains its shape. Leave the flowers for the required time until they are brittle and dry. Take great care when removing the flowers from the powder.

Drying grasses

Tie grasses into tight bundles (they shrink during drying) and hang them heads downwards in a cool, dark place,

Pressing separate petals

In many cases, a far prettier effect in collage is achieved if petals are pulled off flowers for pressing and then reassembled when dried and pressed.

Decorations with whole flowers

Table arrangements using whole dried flowers can be made on a base of styrofoam or plasticine, but some of the easiest decorations to make with dried flowers and grasses are hanging ornaments. These are best made with a styrofoam centre which is lightweight. Use a ball of styrofoam and tie it in halves and then quarters with coloured string or ribbon, leaving the ends for hanging. Fix a ribbon bow at the base with a long pin and then fill in the four quarters of the ball with dried flowers and seedheads. Should some of the flowers prove difficult to insert by their stems, pin them in place through the head of the flower into the foam.

Slightly more delicate in appearance are stars with cone centres, in which grasses or flower stalks are glued to the scales of a pine or larch-cone. Alternatively, a small cardboard disc can be used as a centre, and with combinations of sycamore seeds, oat grains and dried flowers and grasses glued to both surfaces. Gilded or coloured, they make pretty Christmas decorations. Thistles can also be used as a base for hanging ornaments and so can hogweed, acorn-cups and yarrow-stalks.

Ideas using pressed flowers

Besides collage pictures, lovely accessories for the home and gifts can be made using pressed flowers. The finger plates illustrated in this chapter are a charming example.

To make finger plates, cut white cardboard to the size of a perspex finger plate and position the flowers and stalks. Stick the flowers down in the way described and cover with the perspex plate.

Matchboxes with a flower decorated top make acceptable gifts. Arrange small flowers and leaves on the lid of a large box previously covered with white paper and stick them down. Place a piece of adhesive plastic sheeting over the flowers, smoothing it down carefully. Once in position the adhesive plastic cannot be removed, and one should make sure that the flowers are firmly in position before applying it. Larger surfaces can be treated in the same way (notebooks, calendars and greeting cards, for example).

Another idea particularly suitable for the use of pressed flowers is a set of table

▲ *'Iceberg' flower collage. White rose petals were used for the two central flowers*

mats. Make them in sets, and to any dimensions, with a backing of colourful felt or tweed. The top surface of the mat is glass, cut to size by a glazier, in a 24oz or 32oz thickness which will resist the heat of all but the very hottest dinner plates. The edges of the mat are finally sealed with adhesive tape chosen in a colour that seems most suitable.

Collages with pressed flowers

Pressed flower collage is a most absorbing and creative craft, the petals, flower heads, stems, grasses and seeds forming an integral part of the composition itself. The theme of the collage may be more than a design of pressed flowers; it can become a picture, the shapes of leaves and flowers themselves providing the inspiration.

A latex based adhesive is best for sticking down flowers and petals. Choose one which is easily removed when it is rubbed off with a finger and leaves no stain on the paper. A soft paint brush is ideal for lifting petals and for arranging them in position. Tweezers are not recommended because they can damage the flowers. Always use adhesive sparingly in dried flower collage.

Knitting design/darts and shaping

Darts worked for front shaping

Darts worked from waist and shoulder to reduce fullness, method 1

As well as being able to work out their own simple knitwear designs, many knitters enjoy adapting commercial patterns to their personal needs.
This chapter is about enlarging patterns and working darts for waistlines, shoulders and bust shaping.

Obviously to adapt a 38 inch bust pattern to fit a 40 inch bust size two inches must be added across the chest, one inch to the front piece and one to the back, but without experience it is difficult to know what other alterations need to be made to cope with the additional stitches. Although bust, waist and hips measurements can increase by as much as two inches per size, the shoulder width measurement remains almost the same, increasing by only $\frac{1}{4}$ inch per size. For this reason, stitches added to increase a bust measurement, for instance, have to be reduced between the beginning of the armhole and the shoulder line. It is inadvisable to increase the width of the shoulder line to cope with any of these extra stitches, except by perhaps one or two stitches, which can be added to the width of the neck on both back and front without spoiling the garment fit.
To give some examples: if six stitches are to be added to the front of a sweater, one extra stitch can be added to each shoulder, leaving four stitches to be worked into the armhole, two each side. For a set-in sleeve, it is advisable to cast

off one stitch extra at the beginning of the armhole and decrease one stitch extra at the end of the curved armhole shaping. If eight stitches are to be added, two of the stitches can be added to the width of the neck on both back and front, either as stitches to be cast off or left on the holder. The remaining six are reduced as before.
The side seam length of the back and front of a garment usually remains the same in a size increase although the armhole itself increases by $\frac{1}{4}$ inch on both back and front pieces. Because the armhole has been altered, the sleeve head itself also has to be altered slightly, but it is inadvisable to add more than two or three stitches to the head shaping or a baggy sleeve will result; the measurement of the upper arm varies only very slightly in size and, as knitted fabric is pliable, it is better to stretch the sleeve head slightly when sewing it into the armhole.
Although the upper sleeve may require the addition of stitches, it is unlikely that many extra stitches will be required at the wrist, and this fact will alter the number of increases to be worked on the length between cuff and underarm. This means that the number of rows between increases must be re-calculated and altered if necessary. Whether on the body of the garment or on the sleeve, carefully measuring and recalculating is the only sure method of producing a well fitting garment. When altering pattern sizes, think

alterations out carefully and consider the effects of the change on other sections—facings, collars, etc.

Front shaping on knitted garments
Knitted fabrics are so pliable and elastic that fronts of knitted garments are usually made without any different shaping from the back. Because of the characteristics of the fabric this is possible, although it is not the best way of obtaining a perfect garment. Knitting instructions in printed form, whether in a leaflet or a magazine, are written to take up as little space as possible, and for this reason the words 'Front—work as for Back', are given rather than detailed instructions for placing and working waist, bust or shoulder darts. When planning ones own designs, written instructions are not a consideration and front shaping can therefore be included in the form of darts, to give a better fitting garment.

Shaping with darts
Bust darts are usually worked about two inches below the armhole and extending towards the centre. When the point where the dart is to begin is reached, graduated rows are worked, each row being a few stitches shorter than the row before until sufficient have been worked to give the additional length required. Figure 1 shows a possible chart for a bust dart worked over fourteen rows, each being five stitches shorter than the row before.

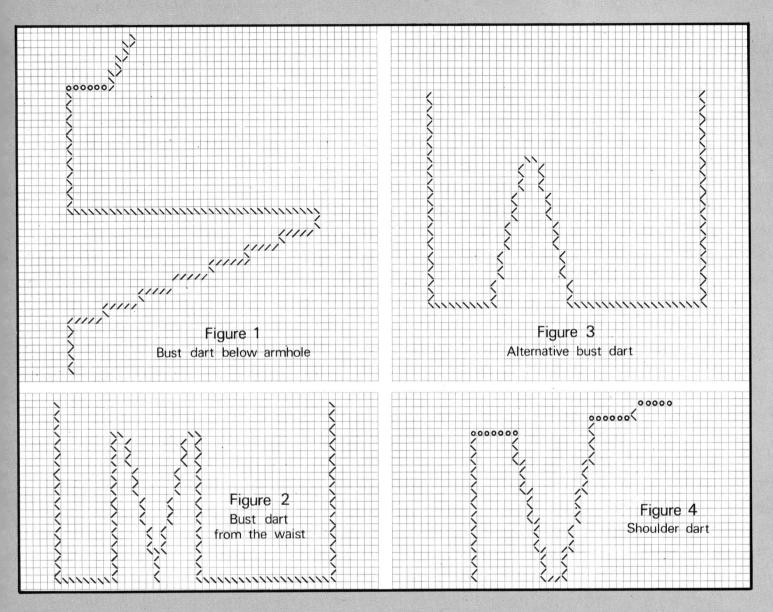

Figure 1
Bust dart below armhole

Figure 3
Alternative bust dart

Figure 2
Bust dart
from the waist

Figure 4
Shoulder dart

Reducing fullness with darts

Where the bust measurement is greater than usual it may be difficult to keep the garment waistline from being too bulky or to reduce a sufficient number of stitches at the armhole. This can be overcome in two ways:

Method 1. Two darts are worked on each side of the front, one running from the waist up to the bust and the other running from above the bust, tapering up to the shoulder line (see illustration).

Method 2. Instead of increasing only at the side edges from the waistline upwards, additional stitches are increased at intervals, usually in a straight line below the centre of the bust area, until the required number of stitches have been worked to give the total width.

Between the armhole shaping and the shoulder line the additional fullness must be decreased and it may be greater than can adequately be dealt with by the armhole shaping alone. By tapering in a straight line, this time upwards, to the shoulder line, stitches are decreased while the correct number for the shoulder are produced.

Both of these methods and working bust darts require a different method of charting because the alterations and shaping take place in the centre of the work and not at the side edge.

Charting darts

When working a dart from the waist upwards towards the bust, decide first on the position of the dart and mark this number of stitches along from the centre front, leave a gap over the number of spaces required for the stitches which are eventually going to be increased, then mark the remaining number of stitches for the waistline on the chart. As work proceeds upwards for the length of dart required, mark the increases on the chart until the gap has been closed. Figure 2 shows a chart for a bust dart from the waistline

where 10 stitches have been increased evenly on either side of a centre stitch, increasing two stitches on every 4th row. Figure 3 shows a different method of charting the same dart.

Although this dart now looks like an opening, the chart is read across the gap, as though ignoring it. Remember that a chart is a map, and not a paper pattern. The shoulder dart required to decrease the fullness will look very similar but will be in reverse as it is decreasing the number of stitches instead of increasing (figure 4).

On the bust dart chart in figure 1 the total side length is the length up to point A plus the length from B to armhole, the rows between A and B do not exist as far as the side seam measurement is concerned.

The lines of increase and decrease may be incorporated into the design, being accentuated by openwork, twisted stitch or even cable panels.

Knitting pattern/long-line jumper

This slimming, long-line jumper has an unusual wide rib which gives a smooth fit, and a patterned yoke and sleeves.

Sizes
To fit 32[35:38]in bust
Length, 26[27:28]in
Sleeve seam, 3in
The figures in brackets [ ] refer to the 35 and 38in sizes respectively

Basic yarn tension
6 sts and 8 rows to 1in worked over st st on No.9 needles

Materials shown here
Jaegar Celtic Spun
12[13:14] balls
One pair No.9 needles
One pair No.11 needles
One set of 4 No.11 needles pointed at both ends
2 st holders

Back

Using No.11 needles, cast on 101[110:119] sts.
1st row K4, *P3, K6, rep from * to last 7 sts, P3, K4.

A close-up detail of the plain ribbing and yoke patterning ▼

2nd row P4, *K3, P6, rep from * to last 7 sts, K3, P4.
Rep these 2 rows until work measures 2in.
Change to No.9 needles and continue in rib until work measures 20[20½:21]in, ending with a WS row.
Next row (patt row) K4, P3, *yon, sl 1, K2 tog, psso, (K1, P1) into the thread between the last st and the next st, K2 tog tbl, move this st back onto left hand needle and slip the next st over it, move st back to right hand needle, yrn P3, rep from * to last 4 sts, K4.
Next row P4, K3, *P6, K3, rep from * to last 4 sts, P4.

Shape armholes
Next row Cast off 6 sts, rib to end.
Rep this row once more.
Next row K2 tog, rib to last 2 sts, K2 tog.
Next row Rib.
Next row K2 tog, K4, P3, work as patt row to last 6 sts, K4, K2 tog.
Working patt row on every 6th row, continue dec at each end of every alt row until 75[82:89] sts rem.
Continue without shaping until armhole measures 6½[7:7½]in, ending with a WS row.

Shape shoulders
Cast off 5[6:6] sts at beg of next 6 rows, then 4[4:7] sts at beg of next 2 rows. Leave rem 37[38:39] sts on holder.

Front

Work as given for Back until armhole measures 4½[5:5½]in, ending with a WS row.

Shape neck
Next row Patt 27[30:33], turn and leave rem sts on st holder.
Cast off 2 sts at beg of next and following alt row, then dec one st at neck edge on every alt row until 19[22:25] sts rem.
Continue without shaping until armhole measures the same as on Back, ending with a WS row.

Shape shoulder
Cast off 5[6:6] sts at beg of next and following 2 alt rows.
Work 1 row. Cast off rem 4[4:7] sts.
Return to the sts on holder, leave 21[22:23] sts on holder for neck and patt to end.
Next row Patt.
Next row Cast off 2 sts, patt to end.
Complete to match first side.

Sleeves

Using No.11 needles, cast on 73[73:82] sts.
1st row P2, *K6, P3, rep from * to last 8 sts, K6, P2.
Continue in rib, working patt row every 6th row and inc one st at each end of every 6th[4th:6th] row until there are 79[83:88] sts.
Continue without shaping until sleeve seam measures 3in, ending with a WS row.

Shape top
Cast off 6 sts at beg of next 2 rows.
K2 tog at each end of every alt row until 47[47:48] sts rem.
Cast off 2 sts at beg of next 12 rows, then 3 sts at beg of next 4 rows.
Cast off rem 11[11:12] sts.

Neckband

Join shoulder seams.
Using set of 4 No.11 needles and with RS facing, work in K6, P3 rib across Back neck sts matching the rib, K up 25[24:23] sts down side of Front neck, rib Front neck sts matching the rib, K up 25[24:23] sts up other side of Front neck. 108 sts for all sizes.
Next round *K6, P1, P2 tog, rep from * all round. 96 sts.
Continue in rounds of K6, P2 rib for 1in. Cast off in rib.

To make up

Press work lightly under a damp cloth and using a warm iron.
Sew in sleeves. Join side and sleeve seams.
Press all seams.

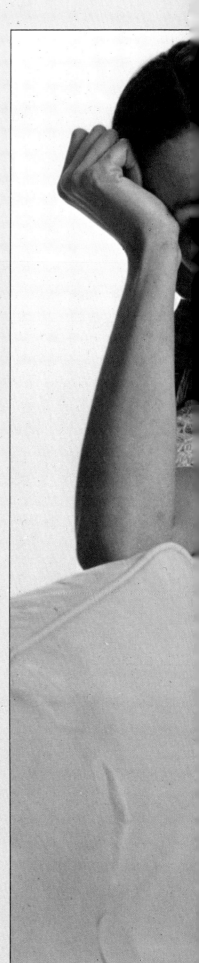

Stitchery pattern/butterfly wall panel

Excluding the frame, the panel measures 21 inches by 10½ inches. To work it you will need:
☐ White linen 24 inches wide by 13½ inches deep
☐ White cardboard 21 inches wide by 10½ inches deep
☐ Fabric adhesive

☐ Anchor Stranded Cotton, three skeins of each colour and four of No.5: **1.** 0131 cobalt blue; **2.** 0168 peacock blue; **3.** 0156 azure; **4.** 0256 parrot green; **5.** 0245 grass green
☐ Blue and green beads
☐ Small blue and large green glass 'jewels'

☐ Beading needle
☐ Crewel needle No.6
☐ Embroidery frame

Working the design
Mark the centre of the fabric in each direction. Transfer the design to the fabric using the tissue paper method and frame

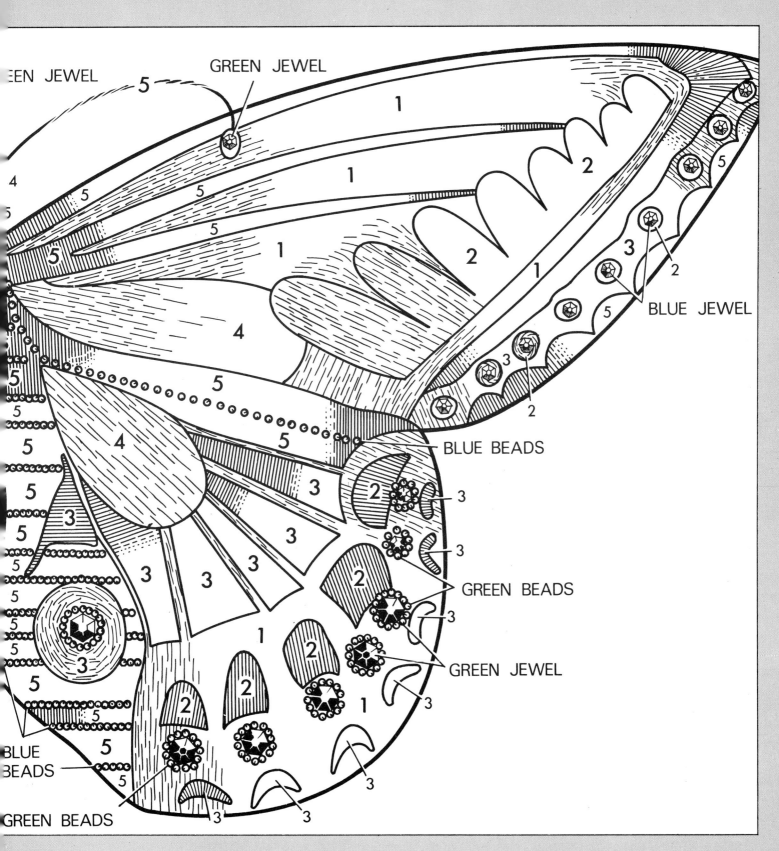

GREEN JEWEL

EEN JEWEL

BLUE JEWEL

BLUE BEADS

GREEN BEADS

GREEN JEWEL

BLUE
BEADS

GREEN BEADS

up. Use four strands of thread in the needle, and following the directions indicated in the outline drawing, work in a free, rather than an exact manner. For the background areas of the patterned wings work split stitch in open rows. Work the satin stitch blocks so that they slightly over-lap the split stitch areas.

Stitch the jewels in position and surround with beads. Fasten the beads upright with a stitch at each side.

Preparing for framing
To avoid breaking the beads, use an extra thick ironing pad. Place the embroidery face downwards and press lightly.

Mount on the cardboard, either by lacing across in each direction with a strong thread, or with fabric adhesive and keeping the horizontal and vertical threads of the fabric in line with the edges of the card. Half of the butterfly and half of the stitch chart is shown, reproduced slightly less than the size of the completed panel.

Stitchery design/flat stitch rugs

This chapter deals with materials and techniques for flat stitch rugs. The next chapter will give the stitches used for pile rugs.

Materials
Canvas. Double mesh rug canvas. The canvas is made from either cotton with 4 or 5 holes to 1 inch or linen with 7, 8 or 10 holes to 1 inch. Canvas with 5 holes to 1 inch is the best size mesh to start on.
Single mesh canvas is also used and the type most commonly worked on is made of closely woven jute with 8 threads to 1 inch. Each stitch is worked over two threads of the canvas. This gives 4 stitches to the inch.
The number of stitches to the inch influences the design. A more flowing and intricate design can be planned on a fine mesh canvas, whereas the same design would have an angular, stepped appearance on coarse canvas.
Wools. It is essential that all wool used is of the best quality and not of a wool/cotton mixture.
2-ply Axminster thrums or hanks are used for the coarse canvas, whereas for finer canvas Brussels or worsted thrums or hanks, and crewel wool are used. For flat stitched rugs allow 6 to 7 ounces of thrums to each square foot of canvas.
Needles. Carpet needles with blunt points and large eyes are used for coarse canvas and tapestry needles for finer canvas.
Scissors. A 6 inch pair of surgical scissors with one blunt and one sharp point is ideal. These must be very sharp.

Designs for needle-made rugs
It is far more satisfying to make a rug to your own design, and the best method is to plan the design on graph paper using each square to represent one stitch.
Before planning a design there are some points to be considered.
A rectangle is the natural shape for a rug. Square rugs do not fit well into most areas. Unusual shapes such as half moons are not suitable for needle made rugs because they waste a considerable amount of canvas; they can only be used in one position and the problems of working a curved edge are practically insurmountable. As a rug is to be used on the floor the design should show up clearly from varying heights and different angles.
The border of a rug should measure at least $\frac{1}{6}$th of the area. For example, a rug measuring 27 inches across should have a border at each side measuring at least $4\frac{1}{2}$ inches. A border is often divided into sections, with one more important border edged on either side with smaller supporting borders. Some motif or part of the main design should, if possible, be included in the border as a unifying link.
When designing a rug which is not being made to fit into a particular area, the normal proportions are for the length to measure $1\frac{3}{4}$ times the width. Always remember when buying canvas to allow for the turn over at each end of the rug and at least $\frac{1}{4}$ yard extra for any alterations which occur when planning the design onto the canvas.

Making a working chart

It is only necessary to make a chart of half the rug design if the pattern has a natural repeat.
Halve the rectangle and mark the depth of the border in lightly with a pencil in case this has to be adjusted later. Plan the motifs on a separate sheet of graph paper and select parts of these to be included in the border. With a free flowing border it is often desirable to have a connecting motif at the corners.
A corner is visually most important and so should be planned first.

Outlining
Outlining the motifs in a design greatly enhances the general effect. This can be done with one line of stitches or, for a stronger effect, a double outline can be worked. Never outline in black as this is too harsh; navy blue or dark brown are more effective.

Stitches
The stitches used for flat rugs are the same as those used for canvas work—cross stitch, long-legged or Portuguese stitch, deep long-legged cross stitch (worked over 2 bars instead of 1), rice stitch, tent stitch (worked diagonally), Soumak stitch, interlocking Gobelin stitch and back stitch, which is used mainly to fill the gaps between other stitches.

Preparation of canvas and edge stitching
Whatever type of canvas is used, the cut edges must be dealt with straight away or they will fray. Fold the cut edges of the canvas over to the wrong side for flat stitched rugs and to the right side for tufted rugs. The turning should be of 2 to $2\frac{1}{2}$ inches for small rugs and a little more for larger ones.
When using double mesh canvas, a double bar should lie along the folded edge to ensure that the large holes of the turned over canvas correspond exactly with those below. Herringbone stitch the top cut edge firmly to the canvas using a complete cross stitch. The other end of the canvas should be oversewn roughly along the cut edge to prevent initial fraying. This lower edge is dealt with as the rug nears completion. If the sides of the canvas are cut then these must be turned over to the same depth and the corners mitred. Do not cut any canvas away, work through all thicknesses for strength.
The next important step is the edge stitching which should completely cover the canvas. The strongest method is plait stitch for all types of canvas, but when working on single mesh jute there are three alternative methods, ie double crochet, blanket stitch and twisted cable stitch. They should be worked between every thread of canvas and about 3 or 4 threads deep.
Before plait stitch is commenced, work a row of oversewing with one thread in the needle along the edge, taking a stitch into every hole of the canvas.

Corners
The corner points are difficult to cover neatly and it helps to paint the canvas in the same colour as the wool being used for the plait. When the paint is dry, work a single cross stitch over the point as an extra covering.
As the plait approaches the corner it should be shortened: when an 'on 3' stitch finishes in the corner hole it should be followed by back 2 on 2, back 1, on 1, so that the last stitch as well as the first along the edge is a simple cross stitch. Oversew the corner point, neatly covering the cross stitch already worked, and commence the plait down the selvedge as before with a cross stitch, the first half of which should be sloping in the direction in which the plait is to be worked. For pile rugs the edging stitch is always worked first, but for flat stitched rugs it is a matter of personal choice. If, for instance, the rug has to be stretched, it is often preferable to work the plait after stretching.

Fringes
These are not really practical as they wear badly and can be a nuisance when vacuum cleaning; however, if desired a fringe may be worked as an alternative to the plait stitch as an edging on needle made rugs.

Finishing
Most flat stitched rugs are improved by stretching, though it is rarely necessary to stretch a pile rug. Stretch the rug face down as for canvas work and dampen thoroughly. The rug should be left stretched for one week to allow it to dry completely. Brass nails should be used to keep the rug free of rust stains.

Flat stitches

Soumak stitch

This is a particularly interesting stitch to work and somewhat unusual in appearance, resembling the weave texture of the Soumak rugs of the East which are woven on a loom. The stitch is worked, as shown in the diagrams, in vertical rows from top to bottom, in horizontal rows from right to left, or diagonally. The working position of the canvas is different from that used for any other type of needle made rug. The rug must be held with the unworked length of canvas laying to the left, and the V which each stitch forms is pointed towards the worker.

Vertical method

Using a single thread in the needle, each stitch is commenced at hole 1 between two threads of canvas (ie splitting the bar).

Insert the needle upwards over two warp bars into hole 2, take it under a weft double bar from right to left into hole 3, and return it to the original starting point at hole 1. Drop it down between the threads of the next double bar to hole 4. The stitch is completed as before to form vertical rows.

Horizontal method

Working from right to left, insert the needle between the double bar to the left of the completed stitch instead of dropping down.

Diagonal method

For a diagonal line descending from right to left, the needle drops down one bar diagonally each time.

For a diagonal line upwards from right to left, the needle moves up one bar diagonally.

In all four methods it must be remembered that each single stitch must be worked and completed according to the basic method instructions.

When using Soumak stitch it is necessary to work a row of back stitch between the first and last row of stitches and the edge stitches to avoid leaving small gaps in the canvas.

When planning a design for this stitch there should be one more hole in the canvas than the total number of squares on the chart.

Interlocking Gobelin stitch

This stitch is quick and easy to do and is worked backwards and forwards in horizontal rows. It is ideal for striped rugs and can be worked across the rug or in lengthwise stripes.

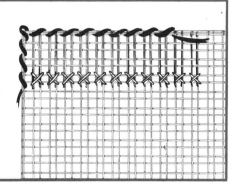

▲ *Corner point and double oversewing*

Soumak stitch—stages of vertical method ▼   *Soumak stitch vertical method completed* ▼

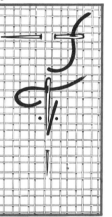 

Soumak stitch worked horizontally ▼   *Soumak stitch diagonally right to left* ▼

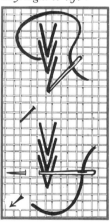

Soumak stitch diagonally upwards ▼   *Working interlocking Gobelin stitch* ▼

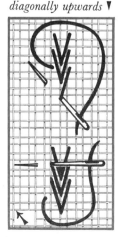 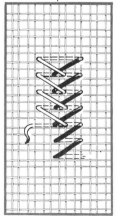

▲ *Detail of a rug worked in Soumak stitch*
▼ *Example of interlocking Gobelin stitch*

Home crochet/window pelmet

This pretty idea from Scandinavia gives an attractive decoration to the top of a window while allowing the maximum of light to filter through. As crochet can be seen from either side the pelmet looks well from outside, too.

Size

Top. Each band measures about 3in (thus 5 bands as illustrated will give a depth of 15in)
Frill. Each scallop measures about 13in wide

Tension for this design
6½tr to 1in over top

Materials shown here

Wendy Invitation Crochet Cotton
About 1 ball for each scallop and 1 ball for the equivalent width of top as required
One No.2·00 (ISR) crochet hook

Frill

Make 20ch and join with ss to form a ring.
1st row 2ch, 17tr into half of ring, turn and work in rows.
2nd row 2ch, 1tr between each tr to end. 18 sts.
3rd row 7ch, *(2dtr, 3ch, 2dtr) between 3rd and 4th tr, miss 3tr, rep from * to end finishing with 4ch, 1dtr into last tr. 5 points.
4th row 7ch, *(3tr, 3ch, 3tr) into 3ch sp, 4ch, rep from * to end finishing with 1tr into 4th ch at edge.
5th row 7ch, *1dc into both 4ch loops of previous rows, 4ch, (3tr, 3ch, 3tr) into 3ch sp, 4ch, rep from * ending with 1dc into last 2 4ch loops, 4ch, 1tr into 4th ch at edge.
6th row 14ch, *1dc into 3ch sp, 10ch, rep from * ending with 1dtr into 4th ch at edge.
7th row 3ch, 12tr into first ch loop, work 13tr into all other ch loops and positioning the 13th tr on the last loop into the 4th of the 14ch of previous row.
8th row 5ch, 1tr between 2nd and 3rd tr of previous

114

row, *1ch, miss one sp, 1tr into next sp, rep from * to end finishing with 1tr into top of 3ch. 40tr.
9th row 5ch, *1tr into 1ch sp, 1ch, rep from * ending with 1tr into 3rd of 5ch.
10th row 7ch, miss first ch sp, *(2dtr, 3ch, 2dtr) into next sp, 4ch, miss 2 sps, rep from * ending with 1dtr into 3rd of 5ch. 13 points.
11th row 7ch, *(3tr, 3ch, 3tr) into 3ch sp, 4ch, rep from * ending with 1tr into 4th of 7ch.
12th row As 11th.
13th row 7ch, 1dc into all 3 4ch loops of previous rows, 4ch, (3tr, 3ch, 3tr) into 3ch sp, *4ch, 1dc into all 3ch loops, 4ch, 3tr into 3ch sp, 41ch, turn, beg at 3rd ch from hook work 1tr into each of rem 38ch, 3tr into same 3ch sp, rep from * 3 times more, **4ch, 1dc into all 3 ch loops, 4ch, (3tr, 3ch, 3tr) into 3ch sp, rep from ** twice more, then rep from * to ** once, 4ch, 1dc into all 3 ch loops, 4ch, (3tr, 3ch, 3tr) into 3ch sp, 4ch, 1dc into all 3 ch loops, 4ch, 1tr into 4th of 7ch. Fasten off.
Work second scallop in the same way until 12th row has been completed.
13th row 3ch, 1dc into edge loop on previous scallop, 4ch, 1dc into all 3 ch loops of previous rows, 4ch, 3tr into 3ch sp, 1ch, 1dc into corresponding point on previous scallop, 1ch, 3tr into same 3ch sp, rep from * to ** on previous scallop, turn, make 9ch, weave first tr strip on previous scallop over and under the 4 strips just worked then work 1dc into top of strip, (9ch, weave next strip in the same way but alternately to first, then work 1dc into top of strip) 3 times but working last dc into top of 2 strips together, continuing along other side of point made by these strips (9ch, 1dc into top of next strip) 3 times, 9ch, 1dc into loop of point on first scallop (the same point as 4th strip was worked from) turn, *4ch, (2dtr, 3ch, 2dtr) into

9ch loop, rep from * 8 times more working into each 9ch loop and into the dc at point where dc was worked into 2 strips together and ending with 4ch, 1dc into 3rd tr on 13th row of scallop, turn, *4ch, (3tr, 3ch, 3tr) into 3ch sp, rep from * 8 times more ending with 4ch, 1dc into same loop as previous row, turn, 5ch, 3tr into first 3ch sp, 1ch, 1dc into loop of first free point on previous scallop, 1ch, 3tr into same ch sp as before, *4ch, 1dc into two 4ch loops, 4ch, (3tr, 3ch, 3tr) into 3ch sp, rep from * ending with 5ch, 1dc into same loop as at previous turn. Continue with 13th row on first scallop, work 4ch, 1dc into 3 ch loops, 4ch, 3tr into 3ch sp, 1ch, 1dc into point loop of plaited part, 1ch, 3tr into same 3ch sp as before, complete as for 13th row of first scallop.
Make as many scallops as are required for the width of the pelmet, joining each as already given. On the end scallops work one set of strips only, leaving the outer edges plain. When all scallops are completed, along the top edge work 1tr, *2ch, miss 2 sts, 1tr, rep from * to end.
Fasten off.

Top section

Make a number of ch divisible by 19, plus 4. Example shown here, 99.
1st row (3tr, 3ch, 3tr) into 4th ch from hook, *miss 2ch, 1tr into each of next 14ch, miss 2ch, (3tr, 3ch, 3tr) into next ch, rep from * to end, 1dc into 3rd of turning ch on frill top edge.
2nd row 4ch, 1dc into next tr on frill top, (3tr, 3ch, 3tr) into 3ch sp, *14ch, (3tr, 3ch, 3tr) into 3ch sp, rep from * to end.
3rd row 4ch, (3tr, 3ch, 3tr) into 3ch sp, *1tr into each of 14ch, (3tr, 3ch, 3tr) into 3ch sp, rep from * to end, 1tr into turning ch, 1dc into next tr on frill.
Rep 2nd and 3rd rows for width required.

Design in dressmaking/more about collars

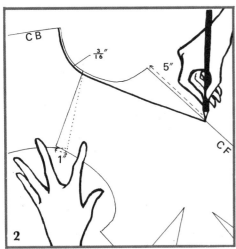

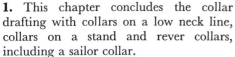

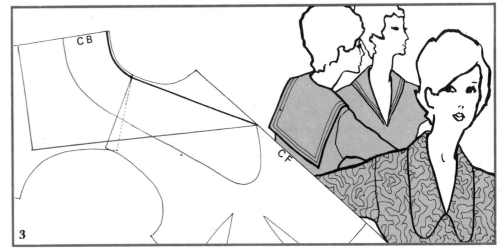

1. This chapter concludes the collar drafting with collars on a low neck line, collars on a stand and rever collars, including a sailor collar.

Some trace patterns for these are given overleaf.

Drafting a collar on a low neck line

2. For a collar on a low neck line, overlap the shoulder seams at the outer edge 1 inch as before. From the centre back as far as the shoulder seam draw in a new neck line for both garment and collar $\frac{3}{16}$ inch in from the original. Then carry on the line to as low at the centre front as you wish—the illustration shows a neck line starting 5 inches down from the neck edge.

Make sure that you will be able to get your head through the neck if you have no other opening.

3. Draw the collar any shape you like and cut out with the centre back fold to the straight grain of the fabric.

Drafting a shirt collar

4. For a shirt collar with a band you will need a ruler.

5. A few construction lines first: draw a line half the length of your neck measurement with a line at right angles to it at either end and one through the middle. Mark one end centre back and the other centre front.

6. Follow the diagrams step by step; written directions would sound unnecessarily confusing (6a, b, c and d).

7. Now draw the 'fall' of the collar as in the diagram (the points can be any shape you like).

8. For a one-piece collar draw the 'stand' parallel to the curve of the collar by using the higher construction lines of the two sets. Extend the lines at the centre front to form the tab of the collar (a). How far you extend them depends on the size of your wrap, or, as the trade calls it, 'button stand'. The top edge of the tab is usually rounded (b).

Mark the position of the button and buttonhole; the buttonhole starts $\frac{1}{8}$ inch to the outside of the centre front.

9. For a two-piece shirt collar, use the lower construction lines of the two sets to draw the band. Extend and mark the tab as before. Extend the neck edge of the band at the centre back and draw in the centre back fold line at right angles to this extension. This collar has a 1 inch stand and a 2 inch fall; you could have a $\frac{3}{4}$ inch stand and a $1\frac{1}{2}$ inch fall.

10. To increase or decrease the size of the collar if you are using the trace pattern simply add or take away from the length at the centre back.

11. The band alone can finish the neck line most attractively.

12. You will not need the usual centre front facings with any of these collars, or the neck band finish. Cut instead a 2 inch turning on the front edges which can be interfaced, stitched and pressed in place before the collar is stitched on.

4

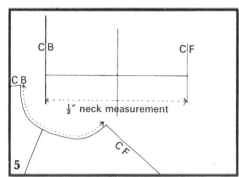

5

½" neck measurement

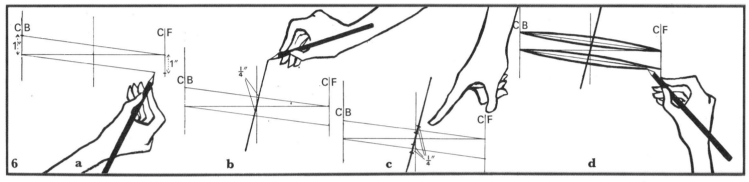

6   a   b   c   d

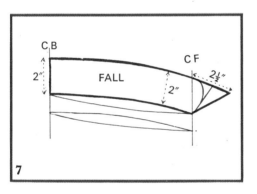

7

FALL

2"   2½"   2"

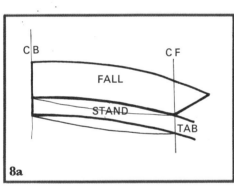

8a

FALL

STAND

TAB

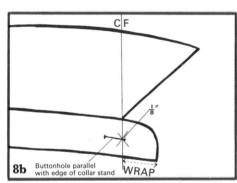

8b   Buttonhole parallel with edge of collar stand   WRAP

⅛"

CF

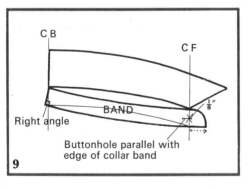

9

BAND

Right angle

⅛"

Buttonhole parallel with edge of collar band

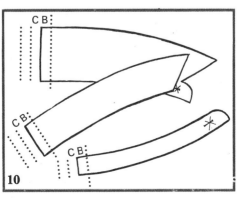

10

11

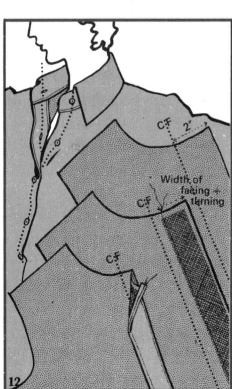

12

Width of facing + turning

2"

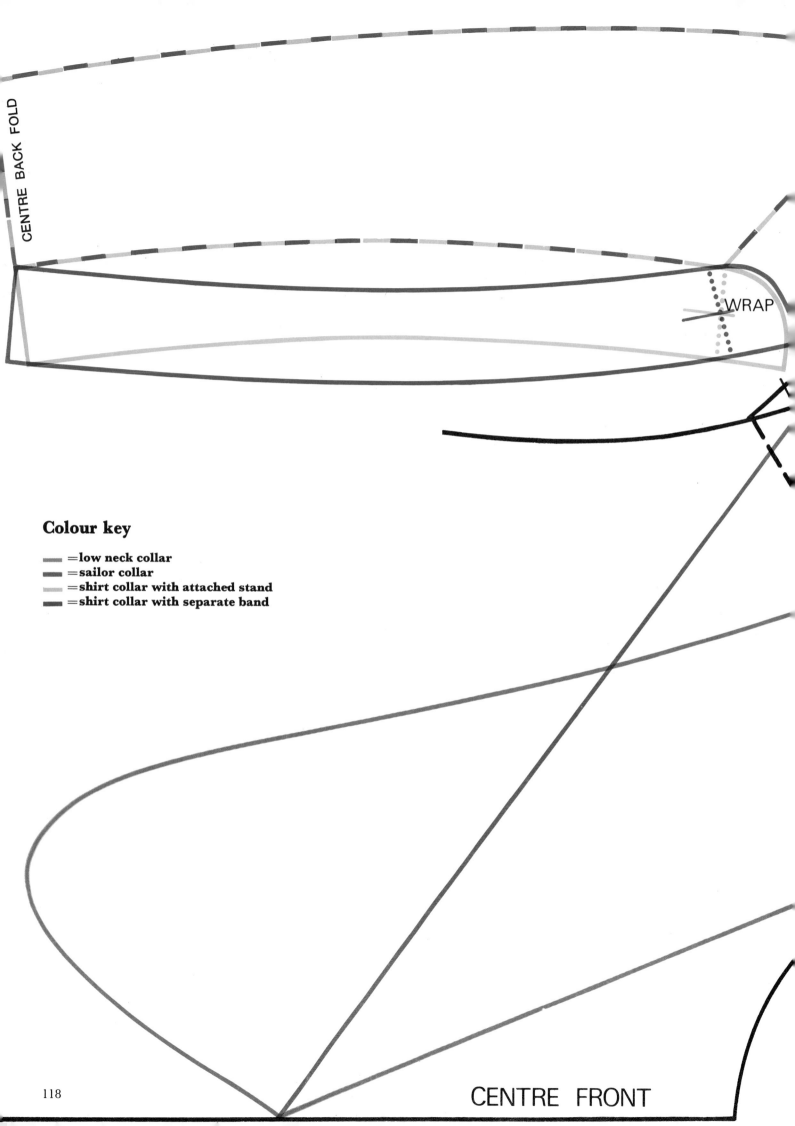

CENTRE BACK FOLD

WRAP

Colour key

━━━ =low neck collar
━━━ =sailor collar
━━━ =shirt collar with attached stand
━━━ =shirt collar with separate band

CENTRE FRONT

To alter the size of the shirt collar see figure 10.

The sailor and low neck collars are altered as for the trace patterns in the previous chapter, figure 12.

CENTRE BACK FOLD

GRAIN LINE WITH CENTRE BACK OPENING

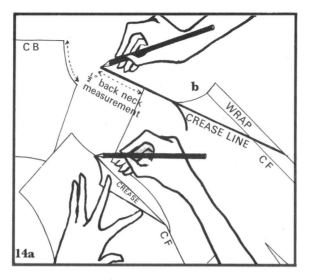

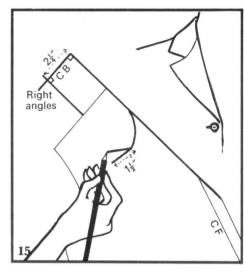

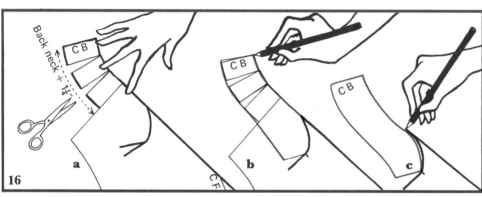

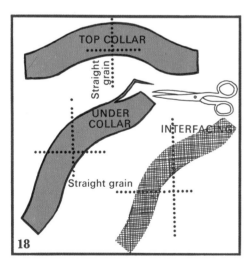

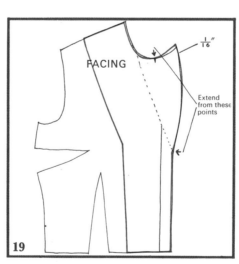

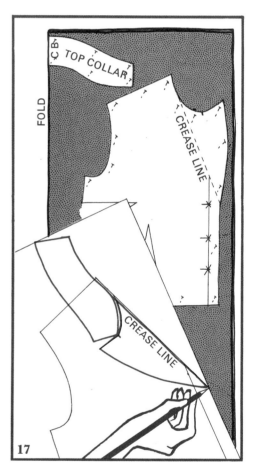

Collar with revers

13. To draft a simple collar and rever use only the front of your pattern. Hold it against yourself and crease it where you want the rever.

14. Draw round the curve before opening the pattern out flat (a). Place the pattern on a sheet of paper and draw in the crease line. Extend the crease line at the front to the edge of the wrap. Extend the other end up through the shoulder point and continue for a length of half the back neck measurement (b).

15. Draw in the 2¼ inch centre back line

of the collar at right angles to the extended crease line, using a set square or book, and draw another line back to the shoulder as shown. To make the notch extend the rever about 1½ inches, then draw the 'notch' of the collar any shape or size you like.

16. Slash the top section twice, from the outer edge, and spread so that the slashed edge measures 1¼ inches longer than before (a). Then draw in the top collar (b). Finally, for a good line on the collar, draw from notch to collar point, making the curve slightly less than the same edge

on the rever (c).

17. Complete the drawing of the rever, very slightly curving the line—it looks better that way. Using the new lines make new front and collar patterns.

18. The under-collar and interlining are cut on the bias, and trimmed away as described in sequel 5, so that the seam will remain hidden. The top collar is cut with the centre back to the straight grain.

19. Use the front pattern to cut a rever facing pattern. Extend it for $\frac{1}{16}$ inch as shown. This will give a good roll to the edge, with no seam showing.

Many people have tried their hand at papercraft at some time or another, either as children, or later when they've attempted to make a paper flower, or perhaps tried to fold a paper napkin attractively for a party table. This chapter is about the art of folding and bending paper to produce three-dimensional effects.

The limitations imposed by using paper as a raw material are in a way an advantage, especially to the beginner. It is impossible to reproduce realistically in paper, so one is compelled to use imagination and originality and interpret what is seen in stylised form.

Once a few simple rules and techniques have been mastered, there is no limit to the wonderful objects and designs that can be made—table decorations, lamp shades, masks, standing figures, animals, pictures in frames, fancy dresses, wall plaques, hanging mobiles—even stage scenery. Paper is surprisingly robust when treated correctly, and creations made from it will last as long they are needed.

Materials and tools

Paper. There are dozens of different types of paper on the market, and it's important to choose one that is right for the work in hand. For a large relief thin mounting card is used, and for a small, light piece of work a good quality thick cartridge

▲ A sturdy London policeman, made in paper for a magazine promotion   *▲ Penguin in paper sculpture designed for a paper company promotion*

paper is best. Anything thinner than this is unsuitable because the paper will not stand up under its own weight, nor will it bend or fold properly. Above all, paper must be of good quality, strong enough to stand well, and sufficiently pliable to bend easily.

Foil-covered and surfaced papers, coloured papers and those coloured on one side only can be most effective for paper craft, although scoring is likely to expose the white backing on the latter. If only white paper is obtainable, and a coloured effect is required, spray-paint the paper before starting or paint the sculpture when it is completed. Never mix white papers in one piece of work unless a contrast is required. There are several different shades of white and one will clearly show against another.

Scissors. These should be sharp. It is best to have two pairs, a large pair for cutting big areas, and a small, pointed pair for delicate, detailed work.

Knife. For a cleaner cut, many people use a blade in preference to scissors, but it is a matter of personal choice. If a blade is used, it must be sharp, and because pressure will be exerted on it a guard of some kind is essential. A stencil knife is ideal. A scalpel blade is also recommended—obtainable with a special holder, or a proper cutting tool with changeable blades. These are all available at craft shops. Razor blades are not recommended because they break under pressure.

Scoring tool. Scoring is an important part of paper sculpture and tools are obtainable from Art and craft shops. A suitable scoring tool can be made by fixing a blunt darning needle into a pen holder, or even by tying one to a pencil

Adhesives. A clear cellulose acetate glue is best for sticking paper. Rubber solution can be used and is easily removed by rubbing off when dry.

Paper can also be stuck together with double-sided paper tape, which is less messy than glue, and can also be used to

reinforce delicate areas.

Ruler. A metal ruler or one with a metal edge on one side is necessary to cut against. Wooden or plastic rulers without a metal edge should not be used for cutting, because there is a danger with these that the knife will skid onto the ruler and cut the fingers.

Set Square. For true right angles.

Compasses. For drawing circles.

Pencils. An HB pencil is probably the best to use. Anything softer will smudge and wear down quickly, and anything harder will make a line that is too faint to see. Keep pencils well sharpened.

Cutting board. Either use a piece of hardboard or an old pastry board but do not use boards with a noticeable grain. Cover the cutting board with thick paper and cut out on this, replacing the paper when necessary.

Handling paper and glue
Cutting. When cutting paper into a shape first mark the line to be cut in

pencil. Then cut against the metal edge of the ruler, cutting evenly and gently three or four times along the marked line until unwanted paper falls away, rather than trying to exert heavy pressure on the knife, and doing it all in one go.

Scoring. Scoring is an important part of paper work, enabling thick pieces of card and paper to be folded without breaking or wrinkling. Scoring is simply cutting half-way through the paper. Mark the line to be cut in pencil, place the ruler against it as for cutting, then cut without exerting very much pressure. With scoring and folding, sharp, clear-cut effects of light and shade can be obtained.

Curling. Sometimes a design may call for a piece of paper to bend gracefully and this means curling the paper. If you are right-handed, hold the paper to be curled in the left hand, and a ruler or a scissor blade in the right hand. Place the implement under the edge of the piece of paper, securing it by placing the thumb of the right hand on top of it. Still holding the paper firmly on the ruler with your thumb, draw the ruler away and towards the edge of the paper. It will curl away from the thumb and down over the ruler or blade (see illustration). Curling gives soft, gentle effects of light and shade.

Applying adhesives

Keep paper, hands and tools scrupulously clean while working and try not to get adhesives on the fingers. Keep adhesives capped when not actually in use and use a spreader wherever possible. A narrow strip of card, cut into four inch lengths, makes effective spreaders for small areas, and a toothpick is also useful for applying dots of adhesive.

An important rule to remember—don't swamp the work with glue; it doesn't necessarily result in a better bond. Two sparingly gummed surfaces left to partially dry will fix quite firmly.

Simple projects

Try the following folds and cuts and observe the shapes and effects which result. Make some basic forms, boxes, hexagons and cones and vary the surfaces with fan pleats. Concave pleats are made by scoring the paper on the surface and convex pleats by scoring on the underside. For rounded shapes give the paper a cylindrical bias by drawing the paper under a ruler before starting to fold and score.

Try each fold and cut and see what effects are achieved. The diagram extreme right bottom illustrates the method for curling paper.

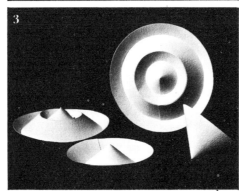

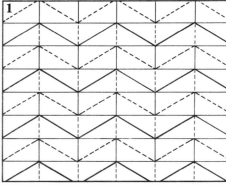

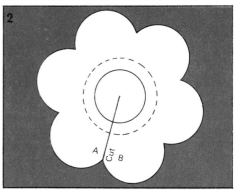

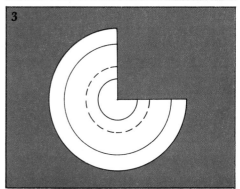

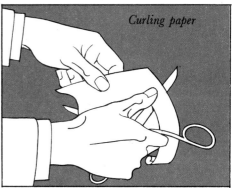

Curling paper

Shadow folds

Score diagonal lines on one side of the paper, reversing it to press in sharp creases. Scoring and creasing are indicated by a solid line for the right side of the paper and a dotted line for the back of the paper. Curvy or wavy folds are made by scoring a reversed curved line followed by a parallel curved line, scoring on alternate sides of the paper.

Different patterns can be made by varying the depth or shape of the folds (figure 1).

Cut surface designs

Cutting into paper at regular intervals gives a design of light and shadow, useful for indicating fish scales, feathers, leaves, etc.

Another useful effect can be created by raising the cuts and placing darker or coloured paper underneath the design. Patterns can be drawn geometrically, but for texture designs such as feather effects they are best cut freely (figure 5).

Cone formation

To make a cone, draw a circle and cut out. Remove a segment and join the edges together. The circle in the diagram has three inner circles, two drawn on one side

(solid line) and one on the reverse side (dotted line). Score these circles and cut out a quarter segment. Bend the scoring on both sides, mould into a cone and secure (figure 3).

Curves

For curves, first draw an 'S' formation and cut out. Score with a knife down the centre, following the shape and mould by bending the scoring to the 'S' shape. This multi-scoring and moulding strengthens the paper, and these curved pieces can be made into many beautiful and different forms (figure 4).

Stylised flower

Draw a flower shape from the diagram, cut out and draw a circle on one side of the paper (shown as a solid line). Turn the shape over and draw a circle slightly larger than the first (shown as a dotted line). Score both circles, one on each side of the paper, and cut between two petals from the outside edge to the centre of flower. Pull 'A' over 'B', covering one whole petal and glue. Crease the centre scoring to make a deep cone. Small flowers are made with only one circle scored in the centre (figure 2).

Knitting design/working up, down and across

The previous chapters have shown knitters how to chart their own measurements and plan their own designs for jumpers, skirts and dresses. The U-necked jumper illustrated is worked on the basic pattern for a sleeveless top and is worked in a three colour Fair Isle stitch. A chart is given to help you to plan the pattern. Work out other patterns of your own.

So far, all the garments in these chapters have been designed to be worked upwards, from a hem or lower edge. Although this is the most usual approach to knitting there are good reasons for considering other approaches when designing garments.

Knitting from the top downwards

Knitting downwards has certain advantages. Skirts worked in this way are more easily lengthened or shortened because the cast off edge is on the hem and it is an easy matter to undo the cast off edge to knit on an extra piece or rattle back to a shorter length. In flared skirts particularly this method of lengthening works well. It is far more satisfactory to add from the hem, continuing to increase until the new length is achieved, rather than adding to the waist with the risk of spoiling the garment.

Sweaters, jumpers and in particular children's jerseys benefit from top downwards knitting. On a child's garment, the wear occurs first through the stretching and breaking of the waist and cuff edges and, of course, the sleeves and body length become too short as the child grows.

In both cases, if the garment has been knitted downwards, the worn edges can be renewed easily with fresh knitting and the length increased as required.

There is an advantage too when working raglan sleeved garments. The shaping of the raglan is formed by increasing instead of decreasing and it can be made to look almost invisible by working downwards from the top. It is a simple matter also to make open work increases, which sometimes look very attractive in a design.

Knitting from side to side

A completely different look can result from side to side knitting worked in simple stitches, and it is often easier to work in colour. For instance, a few rows of a second colour alternative with the main colour is all that is required to produce vertical stripes, difficult to obtain working either upwards or downwards. Skirts, flared or straight, can be most successful knitted from side to side. A skirt can be flared by adding extra rows, turning before the row is complete, repeating with fewer stitches in each row to the required

skirt length, and then working back again until the row consists of all the stitches, much as you would do in working a bust dart. The edge with the extra rows is the flared hem edge. This technique is charted in the same way as for darts in the last chapter. Dresses are too cumbersome to be knitted sideways in one piece but it is possible to make skirt and bodice separately, seaming the pieces on completion.

When knitting side-to-side jumpers or sweaters, it is far more satisfactory to work the fabric for the body first, omitting the welts. When the sections are complete the stitches are picked up along the edges and the welts worked downwards for the required depth.

Designing seamless knitting

Seamless knitting is a little more difficult to design but it can present the designer with great pattern possibilities. For jackets and coats with centre front openings the number of seams can be reduced by working the main section from one front edge, round across the back to the other front edge, with shoulders seamed afterwards and sleeves set into armholes. A jacket can be worked without seams, other than shoulder seams, in two ways. It can be charted from the bottom upwards, working across the entire width of front and back and dividing for the armholes. Alternatively, it can be worked across the width of the garment beginning at one centre front edge and working across back and front, working all the necessary shaping for back and armholes at one side of the work. The other edge is kept straight for the lower edge of the garment. Working in this way it must be remembered that in calculating, the number of stitches gives the length instead of the width, and the number of rows to one inch gives the width and not the length.

Alternatively, a garment may be entirely seamless with sleeves worked circularly and joined at underarm with a circular yoke or raglan shaping. Because of the opening, the sleeves are circular with the entire main section of the jacket worked in rows, although the finished result would be seamless.

Without openings of any sort the garment becomes completely circular in working although each part, whether sleeve, skirt or bodice, retains all the necessary shaping. Circular knitting does not mean that the finished garment will be tubular and shapeless.

Designing diagonally

There are two methods of working diagonally.

Method 1. Where rows are planned diagonally across the work charting can be complicated because of the amount of shaping which is necessary. This is one instance where it is easier to make a paper shape exactly as you require the finished section to be. After calculating tension and the number of stitches required at various points knit the garment shaping as required, measuring constantly against the paper shape.

Method 2. A bias or slope can be given to a panel by increasing at one side and decreasing at the other, thus drawing it across to one side of the work. Again this creates an effect which can be achieved in no other way. It gives a sideways slope to a cable, Fair Isle or patterned panel. This is not easy to chart and again is more successfully worked using a diagram.

Charting patterns

Before attempting to chart in different directions for patterns, experiment with charting where the stitches themselves make the pattern, such as in cable or Aran patterns and in Fair Isle or Norwegian designs where more than one colour is being used to build up a pattern.

The pullover illustrated has a simple Fair Isle pattern worked across the entire width of the garment in stripes. A knitter may want to chart only one pattern repeat or she may prefer to chart the position of the entire pattern to arrive at the best placing of pattern across neck and armholes.

Planning colour patterns

Decide first how many colours are to be used in a pattern and decide upon a symbol to represent each colour. For the pullover illustrated, you might decide to leave a square blank for the background colour, X might represent yellow, and O represent brown. If a lot of colours are being used decide upon symbols as different from each other as possible and mark them clearly on the chart. Different coloured pencils can be used if preferred.

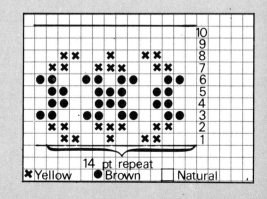

Knitting pattern/sleeveless dress and jacket

This outfit has the simple elegance of uncluttered lines in a smooth stocking stitch fabric. The jacket has bracelet-length sleeves, the dress is sleeveless. Picot edged hems and diamond motifs give the finishing touches.

Sizes

To fit 34[36:38]in bust
Dress. Length, 35[36:37]in
Jacket. Length, 25½[26:26½]in
Sleeve seam, 16in
The figures in brackets [] refer to the 36 and 38in sizes respectively

---

Tension for this design
7 sts and 9 rows to 1in over st st worked on No.10 needles

Materials shown here

Ladyship Siesta Crepe
Dress. 15[16:17] balls
Jacket. 13[14:15] balls
One pair No.10 needles
One pair No.12 needles
5in zip fastener

Jacket back

Using No.12 needles, cast on 125[133:141] sts and work in st st for 1½in, ending with a P row.
Next row K1, *yfwd, K2 tog, rep from * to end.
Next row P.
Change to No.10 needles and continue in st st until work measures 18in from hemline (row of holes) and ending with a P row.

Shape armholes

Cast off 7 sts at beg of next 2 rows, then 2 sts at beg of next 2 rows.
K2 tog at each end of next and following 4[5:6] alt rows. 97[103:109] sts.
Continue without shaping until armholes measure 7½[8:8½]in, ending with a P row.

Shape shoulders

Cast off 6 sts at beg of next 8 rows, then 5[6:7] sts at beg of next row.
Next row Cast off 5[6:7] sts, K to end.
128

Change to No.12 needles.
Beg with a K row, continue in st st for 1¼in. Cast off.

Jacket left front

Using No.12 needles, cast on 63[67:71] sts and work in st st for 1½in, ending with a P row.
Next row K1, *yfwd, K2 tog, rep from * to end, turn, cast on 8 sts.
Next row P.
Change to No.10 needles.
Next row K to last 9 sts, sl 1, K8.
Next row P.
Rep last 2 rows until work measures 16in from hemline, ending with a P row.

Shape front edge

Next row K to last 19 sts, K2 tog, K8, sl 1, K8.
Continue dec in this way on every 4th row until work measures same as Back to armholes, ending with a P row.

Shape armhole

Continue dec on front edge on every 4th row as before *at the same time* cast off 7 sts at beg of next row, then 2 sts at beg of following alt row.
K2 tog at armhole edge on following 5[6:7] alt rows then continue to dec at front edge only on every 4th row until 37[38:39] sts rem.
Continue without shaping until armhole measures the same as on Back, ending with a P row.

Shape shoulder

Cast off 6 sts at beg of next and following 3 alt rows.
P 1 row. Cast off rem 13[14:15] sts.

Jacket right front

Work as for left Front, reversing all shaping.

Sleeves

Using No.12 needles, cast on 51[55:59] sts and work in st st for 1½in, ending with a P row.
Next row K1, * yfwd, K2 tog, rep from * to end.
Next row P.
Change to No.10 needles and

continue in st st.
Inc one st at each end of 17th and every following 8th row until there are 81[85:89] sts.
Continue without shaping until sleeve seam measures 16in from hemline, ending with a P row.

Shape top

Cast off 7 sts at beg of next 2 rows.
K2 tog at both ends of every alt row until 39[41:43] sts rem, ending with a P row.
Cast off 2 sts at beg of next 8[10:10] rows, then 3 sts at beg of next 4 rows. Cast off rem 11[9:11] sts.

Pockets

Using No.10 needles, cast on 33 sts.
Work 4 rows in st st beg with a K row.
Work in patt as follows:
1st row K15, K2 tog, yfwd, K16.
2nd and every alt row P.
3rd row K14, K2 tog, yfwd, K1, yfwd, sl 1, K1, psso, K14.
5th row K13, K2 tog, yfwd, K3, yfwd, sl 1, K1, psso, K13.
7th row K12, K2 tog, yfwd, K5, yfwd, sl 1, K1, psso, K12.
9th row K11, K2 tog, yfwd, K2, K2 tog, yfwd, K3, yfwd, sl 1, K1, psso, K11.
11th row K10, K2 tog, yfwd, K2, K2 tog, yfwd, K1, yfwd, sl 1, K1, psso, K2, yfwd, sl 1, K1, psso, K10.
13th row K9, K2 tog, yfwd, K2, K2 tog, yfwd, K3, yfwd, sl 1, K1, psso, K2, yfwd, sl 1, K1, psso, K9.
15th row K8, K2 tog, yfwd, K2, K2 tog, yfwd, K5, yfwd, sl 1, K1, psso, K2, yfwd, sl 1, K1, psso, K8.
17th row K7, (K2 tog, yfwd, K2) twice, K2 tog, yfwd, K3, yfwd, sl 1, K1, psso, K2, yfwd, sl 1, K1, psso, K7.
19th row K6, (K2 tog, yfwd, K2) twice, K2 tog, yfwd, K1, (yfwd, sl 1, K1, psso, K2) twice, yfwd, sl 1, K1, psso, K6.
21st row K5 (K2 tog, yfwd, K2) twice, K2 tog, yfwd, K3, (yfwd, sl 1, K1, psso, K2) 3 times, K3.
23rd row K4, (K2 tog, yfwd,

K2) twice, K2 tog, yfwd, K5, (yfwd, sl 1, K1, psso, K2) 3 times, K2.
25th row K6, (yfwd, sl 1, K1, psso, K2) twice, yfwd, sl 1, K1, psso, K1, (K2 tog, yfwd, K2) 3 times, K4.
27th row K7, (yfwd, sl 1, K1, psso, K2) twice, yfwd, sl 1, K2 tog, psso, yfwd, K2, K2 tog, yfwd, K2, K2 tog, yfwd, K7.
29th row K8, (yfwd, sl 1, K1, psso, K2) twice, yfwd, sl 1, K1, psso, K1, (K2 tog, yfwd, K2) twice, K6.
31st row K9, yfwd, sl 1, K1, psso, K2, yfwd, sl 1, K1, psso, K3, (K2 tog, yfwd, K2) twice, K7.
33rd row K10, yfwd, sl 1, K1, psso, K2, yfwd, sl 1, K1, psso, K1, (K2 tog, yfwd, K2) twice, K8.
35th row K11, yfwd, sl 1, K1, psso, K2, yfwd, sl 1, K2 tog, psso, yfwd, K2, K2 tog, yfwd, K11.
37th row K12, yfwd, sl 1, K1, psso, K2, yfwd, sl 1, K1, psso, K1, K2 tog, yfwd, K12.
39th row K13, yfwd, sl 1, K1, psso, K3, K2 tog, yfwd, K13.
41st row K14, yfwd, sl 1, K1, psso, K1, K2 tog, yfwd, K14.
43rd row K15, yfwd, sl 1, K2 tog, psso, yfwd, K15.
45th row K16, yfwd, sl 1, K1, psso, K15.
46th row P.
Work 4 more rows st st.
Next row K1, *yfwd, K2 tog, rep from * to end.
Change to No.12 needles and beg with a P row, continue in st st for ¾in.
Cast off.

Dress back

Using No.12 needles, cast on 151[159:167] sts.
Work in st st for 1½in, ending with a P row.
Next row K1, *yfwd, K2 tog, rep from * to end.
Next row P.
Change to No.10 needles.
Continue in st st for 6½[7:7½] in, ending with a P row.
Next row K12[13:14], sl 1, K1, psso, K28[30:32], sl 1, K1, psso, K63[65:67], K2 tog,

K28[30:32], K2 tog, K12[13:14].

Work 15 rows.

Next row K12[13:14], sl 1, K1, psso, K27[29:31], sl 1, K1, psso, K61[63:65], K2 tog, K27[29:31], K2 tog, K12 [13:14].

Continue dec in this way on every 16th row until 127[135:143] sts rem, then on every 8th row until 119[127:135] sts rem.

Continue without shaping until work measures 28[28½:29]in from hemline, ending with a P row.

Shape armholes

Cast off 7 sts at beg of next 2 rows, then 2 sts at beg of next 4 rows.

K2 tog at both ends of next and following 7[8:9] alt rows. 81[87:93] sts.

Continue without shaping until armhole measures 3[3½:4]in, ending with a K row.

Next row P38[41:44], K2, K2 tog, K1, P to end.

Next row K40[43:46], turn, leave rem sts on holder.

Next row K2, P to end.

Keeping 2 sts at inside edge in g st, continue without shaping until armhole measures 7[7½:8]in, ending with a WS row.

Shape shoulder

Cast off 6 sts at beg of next and following 2 alt rows.

Cast off 6[7:8] sts at beg of following alt row.

Leave rem 16[18:20] sts on holder.

With RS facing, rejoin yarn to first set of sts put on holder and K to end.

Next row P to last 2 sts, K2.

Continue to match first side.

Dress front

Work as given for Back until work measures 26[26½:27]in from hemline, ending with a P row.

Next row K58[62:66], K2 tog, yfwd, K59[63:67].

Next row P.

Next row K57[61:65], K2 tog, yfwd, K1, yfwd, sl 1, K1, psso, K57[61:65].

Continue to work centre sts in

patt as on Pocket until work measures the same as Back to armholes, ending with a P row.

Shape armholes

Keeping centre sts in patt correct, shape armholes as on Back.

Continue without shaping until the 46 rows of diamond patt have been completed.

Continue without shaping until armholes measure 5[5½:6]in. End with a P row.

Shape neck

Next row K29[31:33], turn, leave rem sts on holder.

Cast off 2 sts at beg of next row.

Dec one st at neck edge on every alt row until 24[25:26] sts rem.

Continue without shaping until armhole measures the same as on Back, ending with a P row.

Shape shoulder

Cast off 6 sts at beg of next and following 2 alt rows.

P 1 row. Cast off rem 6[7:8] sts.

With RS facing, leave first 23[25:27] sts on holder for neck, rejoin yarn and K to end.

Complete to match first side.

Neckband

Join shoulder seams.

Using No.12 needles, K sts of left back neck, K up 20[21:22] sts down side of front neck, K front neck sts, K up 20[21:22] sts up other side of front neck, K sts of right back neck.

Keeping 2 sts at each end g st, continue in st st for ¾in, ending with a WS row.

Next row K3, *yfwd, K2 tog, rep from * to last 2 sts, K2.

Continue in st st for a further ¾in. Cast off.

Armhole borders

Using No.12 needles and with RS facing, K up 107[115:123] sts round armhole.

Continue in st st for ¾in, ending with a P row.

Work row of holes as before then continue in st st for a further ¾in. Cast off.

▲ *A pretty dress and jacket for day wear* ▼ *Detail of the motif*

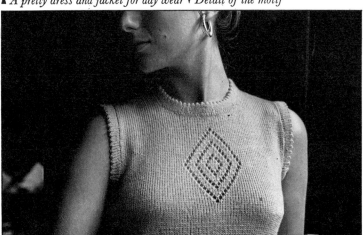

To make up

Press work under a damp cloth and using a warm iron.

Jacket. Join shoulder seams. Join side and sleeve seams and set in sleeves. Turn up hems and slip stitch in place.

Turn in front facing and back neck facing and slip stitch in place. Turn in hems at top of pockets and slip stitch in place. Sew on pockets. Press all seams. **Dress.** Join side seams. Turn in hems and slip stitch in place. Sew in zip. Press all seams.

Stitchery design/pile stitches

The technique of carpet knotting filtered into England from the East during the 16th century. Turkey knot was used on seats and chair-backs.

Canvas and yarn
Work stitches on double mesh canvas with 4 holes to 1 inch. Use 2-ply Axminster thrums, 4 strands in needle for pile and 3 strands for rows of flat stitching.

Method of working
Separate each row of Surrey stitch with rows of deep long-legged cross stitch.
Work three rows of deep long-legged cross stitch for a 2 inch pile and four rows for a 2½ inch pile. To prevent pulling the canvas out of shape work the rows of deep long-legged cross stitch in opposite directions. Work long-legged cross stitch over 4 holes of the canvas at each end of every pile row to prevent the pile of the rug hanging over the edge. When the first pile row is worked, the cut pile should just reach the edge of the rug. Work one row of long-legged cross stitch after the final pile row is completed.

Surrey stitch
Work this stitch in rows from left to right and pull each stitch tightly to form a knot. To change colour, cut end of wool to same length as previous stitch and work next stitch in the new colour. When each row is completed, cut the loops, ensuring that the ends are of equal length.

Turkey or Ghiordes knot stitch
This stitch is worked in rows from Left to right and forms a pile similar to that of Surrey stitch.

Method of working a pile rug
Work plait stitch edging on a pile rug before working the main part. A single row of long-legged cross stitch is usually worked between the pile and the edge stitch.
A pile rug is commenced at the bottom left-hand corner and stitched in rows across the canvas from selvedge to selvedge, working away from the worker. As the stitched area of the rug grows, roll it up out of the way.

Yarn quantities for pile rugs
Use Axminster 2-ply thrums double on 5s canvas; Brussels wool double on 7s canvas and Brussels wool single on 10s canvas.
Rya type rugs require 10-12 ounces per square foot.
The pile rugs use the same quantities as given for flat stitch rugs in the previous chapter.

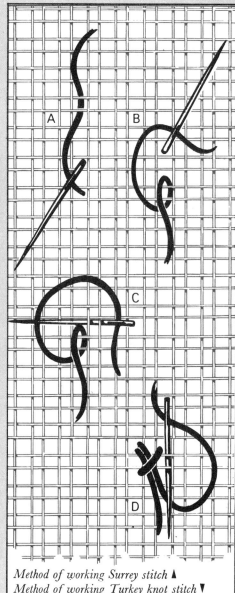

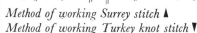

Method of working Surrey stitch ▲
Method of working Turkey knot stitch ▼

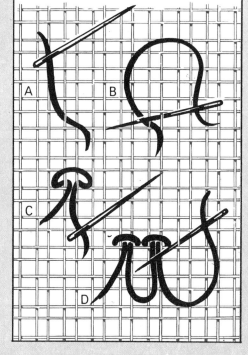

Detail of a needle made Rya rug ▲
Long-legged stitch separating pile stitches ▼

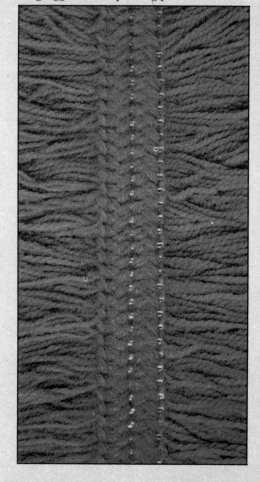

▲ *Modern interpretation of a Persian rug*   *Detail of the rug* ▼   *A back view of the rug* ▼

Stitchery pattern/flowered bedspread

To make the bedspread measuring about 80 inches by 100 inches you will need:
- [ ] 4½ yards 54 inch wide heavy woollen fabric, or a ready made bedspread
- [ ] Pieces of light weight woollen fabric in the following colours and amounts: ½ yard dark pink, ⅝ yard pink, 1½ yards green, 2 yards dark green
- [ ] Sewing cotton
- [ ] Crewel needle No.8

To make the bedspread

Cut the 4½ yard length of fabric in half making two 2¼ yard lengths. Cut one of these lengths in half along the crease line of the fabric. With a flat fell seam join a narrow panel to either side of the wide panel.
Press well.

To decorate

Spread the bedspread out flat. Make a template and cut out flowers and leaves from the coloured fabrics. Arrange them on the bedspread and pin them down. Tack in place and link the flowers and leaves with curving stems cut from scraps of fabric. Alternatively, stems could be embroidered if desired.
Using a zigzag stitch on the machine, stitch round the shapes. If preferred, the shapes can be cut with narrow turnings, the raw edges turned and tacked to the wrong side. Then apply to the background with a slip stitch or fine hemming stitches. Finish the edges with a 1 inch deep bias cut border in the dark green fabric.

Alternative techniques

The simple flower and leaf shapes could also be worked in machine embroidery for a different effect.
Crewel wool embroidery would be effective too, using long and short stitches and French knots. For a combination of appliqué and surface embroidery techniques, work the flowers in chain stitch, working large stitches round and round to the centre of the petals. The stems could be made of flat braid applied to the surface.

Same size template shapes for the flower and leaves

132

Crochet pattern/five bright cushions

These five crochet cushion covers are bright and gay enough to bring sparkle to any room. They are made with a simple background and four of them have modern appliquéd flower motifs.

Sizes
Round cushion. 19in diameter
Rectangular cushion. 19in by 24in

Tension for these designs
4tr to 1in on No.4·50 hook

Materials shown here
Listers Lavenda 4-ply
Round cushion with tassel.
4oz orange, A
Round cushion with flower.
1oz orange, A
4oz white, B

134

1oz brown, C
White rectangular cushion.
9oz white, B
1oz terracotta, D
Terracotta rectangular cushion.
1oz orange, A
1oz white, B
9oz terracotta, D
Orange rectangular cushion. 7oz orange, A
1oz white, B
1oz brown, C
For all cushions. One No.4·50 (ISR) crochet hook (excepting Round cushion with tassel)
One No.3·00 (ISR) crochet hook

Round cushion with tassel

Using No.3·00 hook and A, make 8ch. Join with ss into ring.

1st round 2ch to count as first tr, 21tr into ring, ss into 2nd ch.
2nd round 4ch to count as first dtr, 1dtr into same st, 2dtr into each st to end, ss into 4th ch.
3rd round 4ch to count as first dtr, 1dtr into each st, ending with ss into 4th ch.
4th round 5ch to count as first dtr and 1ch, *1dtr into next st, 1ch, rep from * to end, ss into 4th of 5ch.
5th round 6ch, *1dtr into next st, 2ch, rep from * to end, ss into 4th of 6ch.
6th round 7ch, *1dtr into next st, 3ch, rep from * to end, ss into 4th of 7ch.
7th round As 6th.
8th round 8ch, *1dtr into next st, 4ch, rep from * to end, ss into 4th of 8ch.
Continue in this way, working one more ch between darts on

every alt round until work measures 19in diameter. Fasten off.
Make a second piece in the same way.
Press work under a damp cloth, using a warm iron.
Join the two pieces leaving an opening for cushion.
Make 2 tassels and sew one to centre of each side.

Round cushion with flower

Using No.3·00 hook and B, make 2 pieces as for Round cushion with tassel.
Press work and join the pieces.

Flower centre
Using No.4·50 hook and C, make 4ch and join with ss into ring.
1st round 1ch, 5dc into ring, ss into first ch.

2nd round 1ch, 1dc into first st, 2dc into every st to end, ss into 1ch.

3rd round 1ch, 2dc into next st, *1dc into next st, 2dc into next st, rep from * to end, ss into 1ch. Break off C, join in B.

4th round 1ch, 1dc into next st, 2dc into next st, *1dc into each of next 2 sts, 2dc into next st, rep from * to end, ss into 1ch.

5th round 1ch, 1dc into each of next 2 sts, 2dc into next st, * 1dc into each of next 3 sts, 2dc into next st, rep from * to end, ss into first ch.

Continue in this way, working 8 more dc in every round and working one more round B, 4 rounds A. Fasten off.

Petals

Using No.4·50 hook and C, make 9ch.

1st round 1dc into 2nd ch

from hook, 1dc into each of next 5ch, 3dc into next st, continue along other side of ch working 1dc into each of 6 sts then 2dc into last st.

2nd round 1ch, 2dc into first st, 1dc into each of 7dc, 3dc into next st, 7dc, 2dc into next st, 1dc.

3rd round 1ch, 2dc into next st, 9dc, 3dc into next st, 9dc, 2dc into next st, 1dc.

Continue in this way, working 3 rounds B, 4 rounds A. Fasten off.

Make 6 petals altogether.

Sew the petals round the flower centre. Attach flower to cushion. Press.

White rectangular cushion

Using No.4·50 hook and B, make 86ch.

1st row 1tr into 3rd ch from

hook, 1tr into each ch to end. 84 sts.

2nd row 2ch to count as first tr, 1tr into each st to end.

Rep the 2nd row until work measures 38in. Fasten off.

Press work under a damp cloth, using a warm iron.

Fold in half and join sides leaving an opening for cushion.

Flower centre

Using No.4·50 hook and B, make 4ch and join with ss into ring.

1st-3rd rounds As 1st and 2nd rounds on Flower centre of Round cushion with flower, break off B, join in D and work 3rd round. Fasten off.

Petals

Using No.4·50 hook and B, make 5ch.

1st round 1dc into 2nd ch from hook, 1dc into next ch, 3dc into last ch, turn and work along other side working 3dc, then 2dc into last st.

2nd round 1ch, 2dc into next st, 3dc, 3dc into next st, 3dc, 2dc into next st, 1dc. Break off B, join in D.

Continue in this way, working 2dc into first st and second-last st and 3dc into centre st at other end for 2 rounds. Fasten off.

Make 6 petals altogether. Sew the petals to the Flower centre. Make 7 more flowers in the same way then sew to front of cushion placing 3 along top, 3 along bottom and 2 in centre as illustrated.

Terracotta rectangular cushion

Using No.4·50 hook and D, make cushion as for White rectangular cushion.

Flower centre

Using No.4·50 hook and D, make 4ch and join with ss into ring.

Work as for Flower centre on Round cushion with flower working 2 rounds D, 2 rounds A, one round B. Fasten off.

Petals

Using No.4·50 hook and D, make 9ch.

Work as for Petals of Round cushion with flower, working 2 rounds D, 2 rounds A, 2 rounds B.

Fasten off.

Sew the 6 petals round the centre. Make 3 more flowers and sew to cushion as illustrated.

Orange rectangular cushion

Using No.4·50 hook and A, make 85ch.

1st row 1tr into 3rd ch from hook, 1tr into each ch to end. 83 sts.

2nd row 2ch to count as first tr, 1tr into each of next 2 sts, *1ch, miss 1tr, 1tr into next tr, rep from * to last 2 sts, 1tr into next tr, 1tr into turning ch.

Rep the 2nd row until work measures 38in.

Next row 2ch to count as first tr, 1tr into each of next 2 tr, *1tr into ch sp, 1tr into next tr, rep from * to last 2 sts, 1tr into next tr, 1tr into turning ch. Fasten off.

Press work under a damp cloth, using a warm iron.

Fold in half and join sides, leaving an opening for cushion.

Larger flower centre

Work as for Flower centre on Terracotta rectangular cushion working 2 rounds A, 2 rounds C, 1 round B.

Larger flower petals

Work as for Petals on Terracotta rectangular cushion, working 2 rounds A, 2 rounds C, 2 rounds B.

Smaller flower centre

Work as for Flowers on White rectangular cushion, working 2 rounds C, 1 round B.

Smaller flower petals

Work as for Petals on White rectangular cushion, working 3 petals with 2 rounds C, 2 rounds B, and 3 petals with 2 rounds A, 2 rounds B.

Make 4 flowers altogether, sewing Petals to Centres and then positioning on cushion as illustrated.

Press.

Tailoring one/introduction

Tailoring is not difficult but you must work patiently—with a little care the rewards are great. You may well find it easier to make a successful and professional looking coat than a dress, and will be surprised at how few people guess you have made it yourself. In addition you can save a great deal of money and you will have a garment uniquely yours.

A tailored garment should have a fresh look, appearing as though little work and even less handling has been done. This is achieved by means of accuracy, attention to detail, basting, pressing, moulding and fine hand stitching.

How to use the tailoring chapters

At the end of these chapters you will be able to attempt any coat pattern you wish. Each chapter takes you a step further in the construction of a coat, dealing with various alternatives rather than a separate complete coat in each chapter. For instance, in this chapter the coat is cut out, in the next it is fitted, and when it comes to making the collar stage the different types are covered in turn. So, choose your coat pattern and follow the relevant instructions in each chapter. The beginning of each chapter outlines the contents and the main sections are marked as A, B, C . . . etc. An asterisk * in the text refers to the 'Terms and stitches' used, at the end of each chapter.

Numbers in bold refer you to the appropriate diagram.

In this chapter

A. What you need for tailoring: coat fabrics; fabric designs; linings; interlinings; interfacings; padding; pattern and notions; general equipment.

B. Pressing equipment

C. Cutting out: preparing the fabric; cutting out; marking fabric; interlining.

D. Interfacing: cutting out; darts and seams.

* Terms and stitches

A. What you need for tailoring

Coat fabrics

The fabric you choose for making a coat should be as good a quality as possible and not too heavy in weight. The weave should be close and firm, as the looser weaves tend to fray, causing difficulties during construction.

☐ An ideal fabric is an 100% wool cloth made from short wool fibres which are processed to lie over each other in all directions. This produces a soft dense

cloth with a slightly rough look as found in tweeds and flannels.

☐ Equally good is a 100% wool worsted cloth made from long wool fibres which are processed to lie parallel to each other, producing a smooth fabric, usually with a well defined weave as found in suitings, serge and gabardine.

☐ These two are often combined to make some very attractive fabrics.

☐ It is best to avoid those fabrics with a large proportion of man made fibres as they do not always respond well to the techniques of pressing.

Fabric designs

There are many designs to choose from—herringbone, small checks, self coloured, tweeds etc. It is wise to avoid large patterns and checks as these cause matching problems and some wastage of fabric.

Linings

The lining you choose should complement the coat fabric in weight. So it is safer to buy both at once.

☐ Satin: a smooth, soft and shiny lining. Avoid a cheap one as it doesn't wear well. Good for all weights of cloth.

☐ Jap silk: a thin and soft lining, good for light weight cloth, but expensive.

☐ Satin backed crepe: a satin with a crepe finish. A suitable heavy weight lining for tweeds.

☐ Milium: a satin weave backed with aluminium for warmth. Useful in winter coats.

Interlinings

An interlining is used to give body to a light fabric or a loose weave, and to prevent creasing. It is tacked to the back of the main fabric and interlining and fabric are then made up as one.

☐ Mull: a light, woven cotton.

☐ Organdie: an extremely light cotton with a very close weave. Avoid nylon organdie.

☐ Silesia: a heavier weight organdie.

Interfacings

An interfacing gives body to, and helps retain the shape of, a garment. It is placed between the fabric and the lining. There are two groups of fabric used for interfacing.

☐ Mixed fibre hair canvasses: used for all fabrics and containing the following mixtures.

Wool and hair: very springy and non-crease, the best of all canvasses for keeping shapes moulded into it.

Cotton and hair: slightly springy, but can crease.

☐ Single fibre interfacings.

Pure wool: very springy and soft, useful for

the light-weight tweeds.

Linen canvas (or shrunk duck): a soft canvas that will maintain a crease. Used with very light cloths and as a backing for pockets.

French (or collar) canvas: made with warp and weft * threads of equal weight to give firm control to the under collar

Padding

☐ Tailor's wadding: used for making shoulder pads and padding sleeve heads.

☐ Felt or domette: these are used for light padding at chest or back to give shaping without weight.

Pattern and notions

Paper patterns: When choosing a style look for one which has clean, uncluttered lines. The pattern should be fashionable but not so extreme as to be unwearable in six month's time.

As it is not too easy to mould the end of a wide bust dart, choose a pattern with a seam over the bust or one with side front seams and a small bust dart.

Buy your usual size pattern as any extra ease needed will have been allowed for by the designer already.

Stay tape: ½ inch wide linen tape for holding the front seams of coats.

Threads: a variety are used in tailoring.

☐ Silk: used for all hand stitching.

☐ Mercerised cotton: for all machine stitching. Use a 50 for light to medium weight fabrics and 40 for heavy weight fabric.

☐ White and coloured tacking cottons: for tailor's tacks and basting.

☐ Silk buttonhole twist: for handworked buttonholes.

☐ Gimp: for buttonholes (if unavailable two layers of buttonhole twist can be substituted).

Buttons: The choice is very wide, but be sure to choose ones which will suit the coat style: plain for a country tweed, self fabric for a town coat, leather for a car coat, silver or gilt for a blazer.

Good haberdashers will make buttons from your own fabric and if you wish will incorporate leather, silver or gilt for

Here, and overleaf, are a few styles from the wide range of coat patterns available. They have been chosen to represent different style details. Right: Vogue pattern 8112, in blue and white tweed, shows a simple coat with step collar. Far right. Top (and cover): Butterick 5925 in red gabardine has a belt across the back and an inverted back pleat. Middle: Vogue 2573 in tweed. Bottom: coat, Butterick 6518 in checked angora; jacket, Butterick 6528. Overleaf. From left to right: Vogue 2671, Vogue 2222, Butterick 6462, Butterick 6462.

137

an individual touch.

General equipment

☐ Sewing machine: keep oiled and clean. Fit a new needle and adjust tension to give 10 to 12 stitches per inch on the material to be machined. Always test tension on a double scrap of the fabric before machining.

☐ Shears: very sharp to give a good line when cutting out.

☐ Small pointed scissors: for snipping and buttonholes, pockets etc.

☐ Stiletto: for shaping hand buttonholes (**1**).

☐ Sewing needles: 7 to 8 Sharps for felling, tacking, catch stitching and hemming. 5 to 6 Betweens for pad stitching, side stitching, basting, tailor's tacks.

☐ Pins: long steel dressmaker type.

☐ Tailor's chalk: for marking alterations.

138

B. Pressing equipment

☐ Iron: a dry domestic iron, the heavier the better.

☐ Ironing board.

☐ Cotton pressing cloth: used dry with iron or wet where extra steam is needed.

☐ Wool cloth: a fine wool cloth is used to prevent shine when top pressing.

☐ Tailor's ham: for pressing curved seams. This can be simply made:

2a. Cut two ovals of calico or close weave cotton as shown. With right sides facing sew together leaving a 4 inch gap.

2b. Turn to the right side and stuff very firmly with sawdust.

2c. Hem opening to close.

☐ Pressing roll: used for pressing seams open without the turning being impressed into the garment. Made as follows:

3a. Either cover a wooden rod with

blanket, sewing the edge with herringbone stitch*.

3b. Or make a tight roll of blanket, again sewing the edge with herringbone stitch*.

☐ Wooden clapper: for pressing away steam and for making turnings wafer-thin after steaming (**4**).

If you find a clapper hard to come by an old iron or back of a large flat wooden clothes brush will do just as well.

C. Cutting out

Preparing the fabric

To prevent press marks which may occur on woollen fabrics it is advisable to steam-press the length before cutting out.

Unfold the fabric and lay it right side down on a clean blanket, preferably on the floor to avoid creasing.

Steam press all over, lifting the iron each

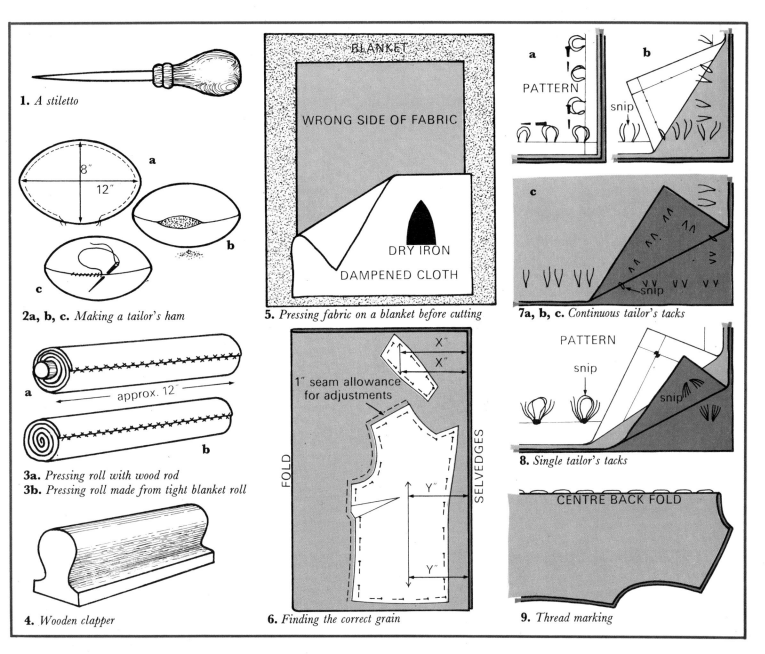

1. *A stiletto*

2a, b, c. *Making a tailor's ham*

3a. *Pressing roll with wood rod*
3b. *Pressing roll made from tight blanket roll*

4. *Wooden clapper*

BLANKET

WRONG SIDE OF FABRIC

DRY IRON

DAMPENED CLOTH

5. *Pressing fabric on a blanket before cutting*

FOLD

SELVEDGES

X″
X″

1″ seam allowance for adjustments

Y″
Y″

6. *Finding the correct grain*

a

PATTERN

snip

b

c

snip

7a, b, c. *Continuous tailor's tacks*

PATTERN

snip

snip

8. *Single tailor's tacks*

CENTRE BACK FOLD

9. *Thread marking*

time. Do not push the iron as this tends to distort the grain.
5. Cover the fabric with a thoroughly dampened cloth and press with an iron hot enough to hiss as it touches the cloth.
Hang the cloth to dry.

Cutting out
Trim the paper pattern to the cutting line.
6. Following the instruction sheet layout place the pattern pieces on the fabric. To make sure the grain lines * are correct measure out equal distances from the selvedge to each end of the arrow on the pattern as shown. Smooth the paper and pin every 2 inches along the stitching line. Cut out carefully. It is wise to make seam allowances of 1 inch at shoulders, armholes and side seams to allow for alterations.

Marking the fabric
Transfer pattern markings to the fabric using tailor's tacks and thread markings. Chalk and tracing paper lines are not permanent enough for tailoring, as accuracy in following pattern lines is essential for a perfect fit.
Always work with pieces laid flat.
Use the following markings:
☐ Tailor's tacking—continuous: used for marking stitching lines.
7a. After cutting out and before removing the paper pattern, mark all stitching lines with continuous tailor's tacks. To do so, thread a needle with double thread and, on the stitching line, make stitches through both layers of fabric and the pattern, a loop being made at each stitch.
7b. To remove the pattern snip through the centre of each loop, unpin the pattern and gently ease the paper away.

7c. Gently pull the fabric edges apart and cut the stitches, leaving tufts on both sides. Mark the wrong side of each piece with a chalk cross.
☐ Tailor's tacks—single: used for marking balance marks and style details.
8. Using a double thread take a stitch through the dot or hole in the pattern and both layers of fabric.
Repeat, leaving a loop.
Snip the loop before removing the pattern.
☐ Thread marking: used for marking centre back, centre front and alteration and style lines.
9. Thread marking is a continuous line through one layer of fabric as shown.
Colour code: if a colour code routine is adopted in this marking it saves confusion later—so tailor's tack seam lines in white and use colours for matching balance points.

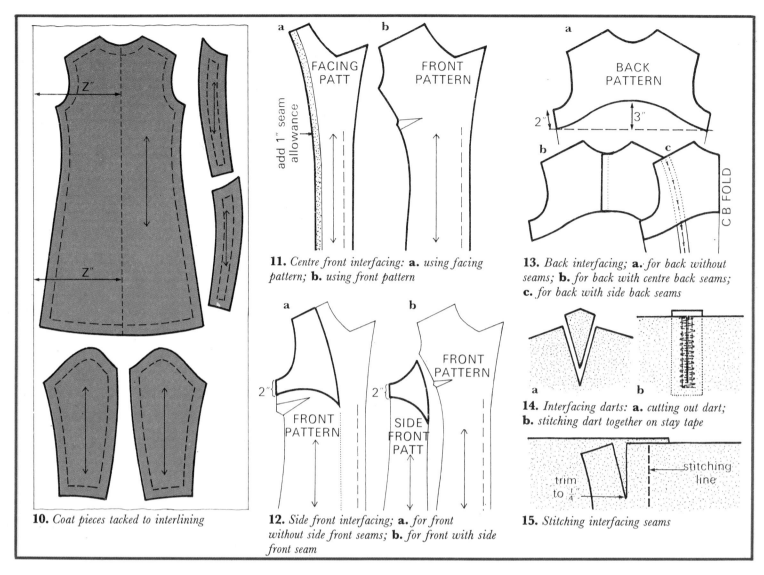

10. *Coat pieces tacked to interlining*

11. *Centre front interfacing: a. using facing pattern; b. using front pattern*

12. *Side front interfacing; a. for front without side front seams; b. for front with side front seam*

13. *Back interfacing; a. for back without seams; b. for back with centre back seams; c. for back with side back seams*

14. *Interfacing darts: a. cutting out dart; b. stitching dart together on stay tape*

15. *Stitching interfacing seams*

Inter or underlining

If it is necessary to interline the fabric work as follows:

10. After the coat fabric has been cut out, marked up and separated, place each back, front and sleeve piece on to the single interlining fabric. Place the wrong side to the interlining, matching the grain. Tack together all round 1 inch in from the stitching line.

Cut out and work interlining and coat fabric as one.

D. Interfacing

This relates to all tailored coats.

Cutting out

Interfacing should be steam pressed before cutting out to prevent shrinkage during shaping.

Coat and interfacing grains should coincide to avoid the possibility of distortion.

11a and b. For each front, cut one piece of canvas as for the facing, adding an extra 1 inch seam allowance at the inner

140

edge (a). If your pattern has a side front seam use the front pattern complete instead of the facing pattern (b).

12a and b. Cut a second piece of interfacing for each front to include the armhole as shown, using the front, or side front, pattern as a guide.

13a, b and c. For the back, cut canvas to include the neck and armhole, using the back pattern as a guide and curving the lower edge as shown (a). If there is a centre back seam cut two pieces of canvas and join them at the centre back (b). Where you have side back seams, overlap the pattern pieces on the stitching line and cut as shown (c).

Darts and seams

There are two ways to give shaping to the canvas interfacings, but you must fit the tacked canvas and coat before shaping.

14. Darts. Cut the dart shape out along the stitching line. Place the cut edges together over stay tape. Machine stitch.

15. Seams. Overlay on the stitching line, machine stitch and then trim the seam

allowances to ¼ inch.

Press the canvas over a tailor's ham to retain its shape.

*Terms and stitches

Grain lines (16): lengthwise grain, or warp threads, run parallel to the selvedge. Crosswise grain, or weft threads, run across the fabric from selvedge to selvedge.

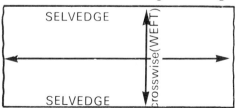

Herringbone stitch (17)

Warp and weft: see grain lines.

Crafts/tie and dye printing

The process and method

Tie and dye is the term given to a process where patterns are dyed into cloth, and it's so simple even a child can do it—and many children do produce beautiful examples.

The craft consists of taking a piece of fabric, then tying, folding, binding, knotting or sewing it so that when the fabric is dipped in a dyebath the colour penetrates the untied areas and a pattern appears on the areas which have been protected from the dye. More complex patterns can be created by using more than one colour, and re-tying first one area, then another. Tie and dye can be worked on lengths of fabric for furnishing, on household linens or on garments. Dresses, blouses, skirts, trousers, ties, pillow cases and curtains, can all be decorated with the tie and dye process.

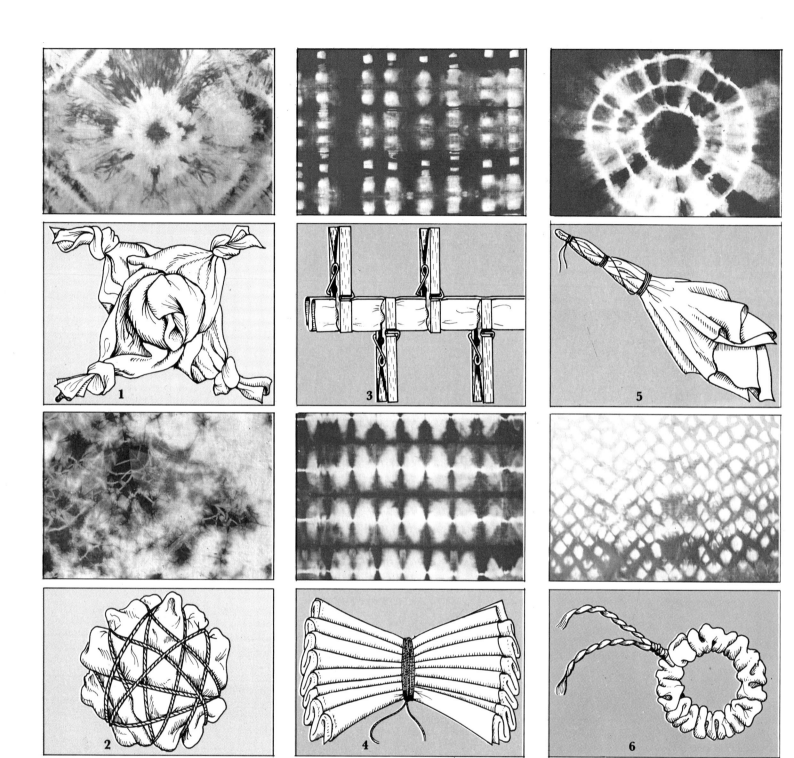

How to make patterns

There are countless ways of tying up a bundle of fabric to produce a design. A picture guide is given in this chapter showing just a few of them and the patterns that will result.

1. Knotted squares. Pick up a point of fabric in the centre of the square, knotting the point and each corner.

2. Marbling. Crumple up the fabric in the hand. Bind into a hard ball. Crumple in different places for each colour used. For a large garment, bunch along the length, section by section, making a long firm roll.

3. Pleat a piece of fabric and secure with clothes pegs.

4. Stripes. Fold a piece of fabric in four, pleat it and then bind with string.

5. Small circle. Pick up a piece of fabric to form a 'furled umbrella' shape and bind with thread.

6. Ruching round cord. Roll a piece of cloth round a length of cord and ruch.

7. Clump-tying. **A.** Bind a cork into a piece of fabric.

8. Clump-tying. **B.** Tie a number of different sized stones into a piece of fabric.

9. Small circle. Pick up a piece of fabric to form a 'flared umbrella' shape and cross bind with thread.

10. Fold a piece of fabric in half and pleat it. Bind at various intervals with string, raffia and thread.

11. Twisting and coiling. Fold the cloth in half, pleat, then twist until it coils back on itself like a skein of wool. Bind at ends and at intervals.

12. Simple double knots.

Experiment and discover which pattern is the most suitable for the fabric or garment being dyed. Marbling makes a pretty, all-over pattern for most things and stripes are particularly effective on towels and curtains.

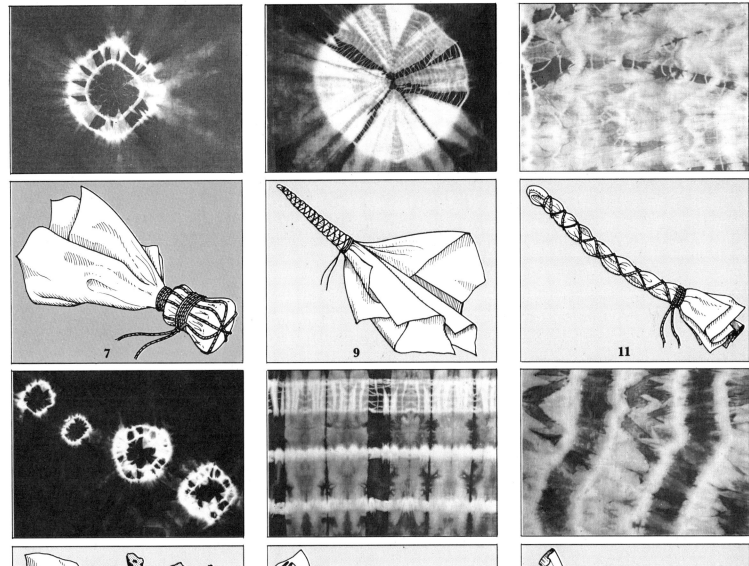

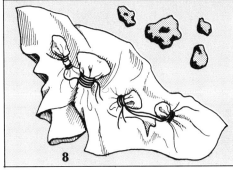

7

8

9

10

11

12

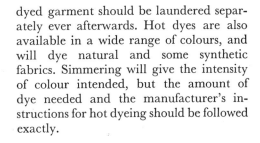

Fabrics and equipment

Cold water dyes will dye natural fibres such as silk, cotton and linen in bright colours. They are very easy to use and the results are wash and light fast. Cold water dyes come in a large range of shades, and one tin of dye is required for each ½lb (250 grams) of dry fabric—ie two to three square yards of medium weight fabric. For example, a dress weighing one pound to be dyed blue and red will require two tins of blue and two tins of red cold water dye.

When fast, cold water dyes are not available a hot dye can be used, but the dyed garment should be laundered separately ever afterwards. Hot dyes are also available in a wide range of colours, and will dye natural and some synthetic fabrics. Simmering will give the intensity of colour intended, but the amount of dye needed and the manufacturer's instructions for hot dyeing should be followed exactly.

Fabrics

It is not advisable to tie-dye woollen sweaters as the tying may make them go out of shape. Woollen fabrics can be dyed but manufacturer's special instructions for dyeing wool should always be followed. Generally, cold dyes are a better choice for woollen fabrics than hot ones.

Fabrics unsuitable for dyeing are polyester/wool mixtures, acrylics (Orlon, Acrilan, Courtelle, Neospun), Tricel and acetate rayon. Fabrics with special finishes resist dyeing and should not be chosen for tie-dyeing. Polyesters, like Terylene, Dacron, and Crimplene, when dyed with triple strength hot dye in dark shades, will come out as pretty pastel shades.

Shirts, linens, towels and anything which is going to need constant washing should be dyed with cold dye, which is colour fast.

143

Other materials needed

- ☐ Salt
- ☐ Soda (for cold dyeing, not needed for hot dyeing)
- ☐ Wooden spoon to stir with
- ☐ Rubber gloves to protect hands
- ☐ Container, big enough to submerge the tied fabric; plastic or glass for cold water dye, a heat resistant container for hot dye
- ☐ Jug to hold one pint (or half a litre)
- ☐ Thread, elastic bands, cork, pebbles, string, raffia, cord, cotton, or anything else needed to make the patterns.

Hints and tips

• New fabric may have dressing in it which will resist dye, so boil the garment or fabric first, ironing it smooth again when it is dry.

• When making tie-dyed dresses, always tie-dye the material first, and then make up the dress. The finished garment will have a much more professional look.

• Tie up a sample piece before immersing the whole piece of fabric in the dye bath. Dye, rinse, wash, and untie it, to see whether the resulting pattern and colour is as required. Don't forget that the colour will look darker when the fabric is wet.

• If an old, coloured garment is to be tie-dyed to freshen it, remove the original colour with colour remover, but test a sample first to find out if the dye is fast.

• When two or more colours are used they will blend with one, another, so choose colour combinations carefully, remembering that red and blue make mauve; red and yellow make orange; yellow and blue make green; and that a lot of colours mixed together will usually make mud!

How to start

Bind the fabric in any of the ways shown in this chapter. Leave two inches of thread when starting binding, and when binding is completed return to the starting point and tie the two ends together. This will help to ensure that the whole thing does not unravel in the dyebath.

If several bindings are being used on one garment, just use a slip knot and carry the thread onto the next binding.

For a sharp pattern, thoroughly wet the item before putting it in the dye bath. For a softer outline, put the item in the dye bath quite dry.

Prepare the dye. Always work the lightest colour first.

For cold water dyes, dissolve the dye in one pint of warm water, stir well, and pour into the dye container. For each tin of dye used, dissolve 4 tablespoonsful of salt and one tablespoonful of common

▲ *An unusual way of using tie and dyed fabrics* ▼ *Four neckties to make*

144

soda in one pint of hot water. Stir well, and when everything is ready to dye, add the salt and soda to the mixture. Once the soda is added to the dye, it is only effective for about two hours, so don't add until everything is ready.

Neckties from sheeting
The four ties illustrated were made from tie-dyed cotton sheeting. Experiment with the knots and colours for different effects.
Tortoiseshell banded tie. Dye colours: coral red and café au lait.
Method: Fold a length of cloth 52 inches long by 7 inches wide in half along the length. Tie as many knots along the length as possible. Dye in coral red, rinse, untie, rinse again. Re-tie and dye in café au lait.
Red ovals tie. Dye colours: nasturtium and camellia.
Method: Fold length of cloth 52 inches by 7 inches lengthwise. Pick up small tufts of cloth along the fold and bind them narrowly, leaving a $\frac{1}{4}$ inch gap between each tie. Widen the tufts towards the end. Dye in nasturtium. After rinsing and while still tied, bind each tuft again below the original tie. Dye in camellia.
Purple chevron tie. Dye colours: French navy and camellia.
Method: Cut two pieces of cloth on the cross, each 28 inches by 8 inches. Fold each piece in half lengthwise. Roll the doubled cloth diagonally into a tube, beginning at the corners and working towards the folded edge. Make narrow bindings at 1 inch intervals along this tube. Dye each roll in French navy. Rinse, and while still wet, add further bindings between the original ties. Let the rolls dry and then dye again in weakly-made camellia coloured dye ($\frac{1}{4}$ teaspoonful of dye made up to 1 pint with 2 teaspoonsful of salt and $\frac{1}{4}$ teaspoon of soda added).
Rinse well, hot wash and rinse again. Make up necktie by joining two pieces together and pointing the ends.
Red kipper tie. Dye colour: Camellia.
Method: Cut two lengths of cloth 52 inches by 6 inches. Fold in half lengthwise. Follow this procedure for both pieces, Pick up a piece of fabric, on the fold, about 4 inches from the end. Pull it into a tent shape and bind diagonally right up to the point, then back to the beginning and tie the thread ends. The tent shape by now should be a finger shape. Leave little gaps in the binding so that as the dye partially penetrates a criss-cross texture is achieved. Each of these bindings will make a circle. Make as many circles as required, decreasing in size towards the centre. Tie from the other end in the same way. Wet the cloth and dye.

Knitting design/trousers and continental patterns

Once the intricacies of charting shapes have been mastered, designing and charting a pair of knitted trousers is comparatively simple. Combined with the garments already given in the previous design chapters, smart two-piece outfits can be designed. This chapter also explains how to work from continental patterns.

Drafting

The main measurements required for a pair of trousers are:

1. The total side length from waistline down the outer side of the leg to the ankle or the required length.
2. The total measurement around the upper hip.
3. The hipline at the widest point.
4. The required width around upper leg, taken 3 inches below the crutch
5. The required width around the leg just above knee.
6. The required width of the lower edge.
7. Length from the lower edge to the top of the knee.
8. Inside leg length from lower edge to crutch.

Trousers diagram

Begin by marking the centre line AB. This is the total side length from waistline to the required length (measurement 1). Using the line AB as the centre line mark on it O, which is the distance between lower edge and top of knee (measurement 7). Mark P on the line, measuring from just above knee to the point where the upper leg measurement was taken. Q is the length from lower edge to the crutch—the inside leg measurement. R is the point at which the upper hipline measurement was taken.

Using AB with the marked points as a centre line mark the following:
CD—half the total waist measurement plus required tolerance ($1\frac{1}{4}$ inch is recommended for this design).
EF—half the upper hips measurement plus tolerance ($1\frac{1}{4}$ inch for this design).
GH—half of the measurement around the hips plus tolerance (for this design $4\frac{1}{2}$ inches is recommended).
IJ—the actual circumference of the upper leg plus tolerance.
KL—the actual circumference of the leg just above the knee plus tolerance.
MN—the width required at lower edge.
The shape of the trouser leg is a matter of design choice. It can be sloped from GH to MN for a flared look or, if the trousers are to have a fitting leg, the lines will slope inwards.
Mark a point S on the chart 1-$1\frac{1}{2}$ inches above point D. This is to give extra

length to the back seam to allow for ease in sitting down. Draw a slightly curved line from A to S. In the same way the centre front point C can be dropped slightly to shorten the front seam, but on knitted fabric, which is very elastic, it is not essential.
The curve from G to C is sharp where it starts at G and curves to E, then it is less shaped to C, much as is found in an armhole curve.
The back curve from H to F can be more gradual.
Draw the diagram to look like figure 1, and this is your working diagram for the left trouser leg. Prepare a tension and stitch swatch and mark in numbers of rows and stitches.
The leg shaping is usually fairly easy to arrange but from the line GH it is easier to work the shaping out on graph paper. Remember that this diagram is for the left leg. For the right leg it is necessary to reverse the shaping above GH to the waistline.
Because of the degree of elasticity in knitted fabric it is quite easy to obtain a well fitting pair of trousers that have no side opening and are fitted with elastic at the waist. A more tailored pair of trousers would be similar from the hipline upwards to a skirt pattern and could have the fullness reduced by darts as well as by shaping over the hipline.

Trousers in circular knitting

Trousers also lend themselves to being worked without seams using circular needles. Each leg is worked circularly and then joined just above the crutch where a small seam is necessary, so that the body is also worked without seams.

Continental type charts

Continental designs, seen in magazines and leaflets, often suggest an idea which appeals to the knitter, but they are impossible to understand if one lacks the knowledge of technical terms in another language. Often, however, foreign instructions do away with the need to understand every word by the clever use of diagrams.
Figure 2 is typical of these diagrams and shows half the back of a stocking stitch sweater, slightly shaped towards the waist with a narrow edge of ribbing, and with the waistline defined by a ribbed panel. The number of stitches to be cast on is indicated under the diagram and in some diagrams this may be for half the pattern or it may indicate that although only half the back is shown the total number of stitches to be cast on has been stated. A quick check as to the tension

one expects to work at and the number of stitches one would therefore cast on will decide this if there is any doubt.
The ribbing at the lower edge is usually indicated by tiny upright lines and may have the depth indicated beside it, ie 2cms (2 centimetres).
The distance between the ribbing and the waist ribbing will have a measurement against it, and decreasings marked by a small dot. Figure 2 indicates one decrease four times in all at each side. To determine the number of rows between calculate how many rows will be needed to reach the required measurement and then divide this into even sections.
The waist ribbing is again indicated by small vertical lines and above there is an area with dots to indicate the number of times increases are to be worked—four in figure 2.
At the armhole, the 3 and 2 indicate that 3 stitches are cast off first. On the next row 3 stitches would be cast off on the

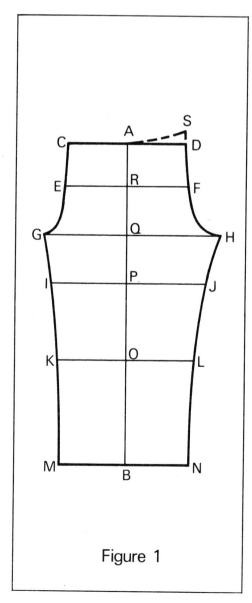

Figure 1

other side of the work and then 2 stitches at the beginning of the next 2 rows. The dots above this indicate again where stitches are decreased and how often they are worked. Close together on an armhole curve they would be worked on alternate rows. In the same way the remaining numbers refer to the stitches to be cast off for neck shaping and the number of times you cast off for the shoulder.

Because a diagram takes up a great deal less print space than row by row instructions many continental designs give more varied methods of shaping than British designs. Apart from sweaters many designs have backs which are narrower than the front. This gives an exceedingly good line when the garment is made up because the side seam tends to be towards the back instead of centrally below the armhole. When measuring this type of design do not simply double the front or back measurement to see if it is the size you require, but add both back and front together.

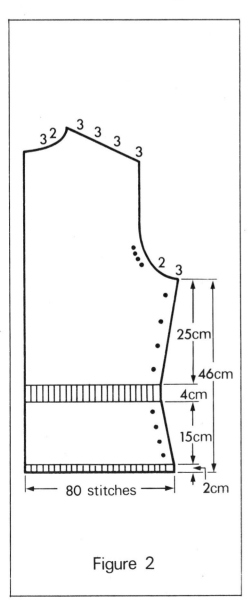

Figure 2

Knitting pattern / striped for two

This bright striped jumper teams with plain trousers or skirt. If you are knitting for a little girl there's double value—the top can team with skirt or trousers. The patterns could hardly be simpler. All in stocking stitch, the jumper has four row stripes, the skirt and trousers start and finish with one inch of ribbing.

Sizes

To fit 21[22:23]in chest
Jumper. Length, 13½[14½:15]in Sleeve seam, 9[10:11]in
Skirt. Length, 9[9½:10]in, adjustable
Trousers. Inside leg, 13[14:15]in, adjustable

> **Tension for this design**
> 5 sts and 7 rows to 1in over st st worked on No.7 needles

Materials shown here

Hayfield Courtier Super Crimp Bri Nylon Double Knitting
Jumper. 4[4:4] balls main shade, A, red
4[4:4] balls contrast, B, white
Skirt. 4[5:6] balls A, red
Trousers. [4:5] balls A, red
One pair No.7 needles
One pair No.9 needles
One set of 4 No.9 needles pointed at both ends
Waist length elastic for trousers
2 buttons for skirt
Stitch holder

Jumper back

Using No.9 needles and A, cast on 53[55:57] sts.
1st row K1, *P1, K1, rep from * to end.
2nd row P1, *K1, P1, rep from * to end.
Rep these 2 rows once more, inc 5[5:6] sts evenly across the 2nd row. 58[60:63] sts.
Change to No.7 needles and join in B.
Continue in st st working 4 rows B, 4 rows A throughout until work measures 8½[9:9½]in from beg. End with a WS row.

Shape armholes

Cast off 2 sts at beg of next 2 rows.
148

Next row K1, sl 1, K1, psso, K to last 3 sts, K2 tog, K1.
Continue dec in this way on every 4th row 2[2:3] times more, then on every alt row until 24[24:27] sts rem.
End with P row.
Leave sts on holder.

Front

Work as given for Back until 34[34:37] sts rem. End with P row.

Shape neck

Next row K1, sl 1, K1, psso, K6, turn and leave rem sts on st holder.
Next row P to end.
Next row K1, sl 1, K1, psso, K to last 2 sts, K2 tog.
Rep the last 2 rows twice more, then the first of these 2 rows once more.
Next row K1, sl 1, K2 tog, psso.
Next row P2 sts.
Next row K2 tog. Fasten off.
Return to sts on holder. Leave first 16[16:19] sts on holder for neck, K to last 3 sts K2 tog, K1.
Complete to match first side.

Sleeves

Using No.9 needles and A, cast on 25[27:29] sts and work in rib as given for Back for 2in, ending with a WS row and inc 8 sts evenly across last row. 33[35:37] sts.
Change to No.7 needles and join in B.
Continue in st st working in stripes of 4 rows B, 4 rows A throughout, inc one st at each end of every 8th row until there are 41[43:45] sts.
Continue without shaping until sleeve seam measures about 9[10:11]in from beg, ending with the same row as Back at armholes.

Shape top

Cast off 2 sts at beg of next 2 rows.
Next row K1, sl 1, K1, psso, K to last 3 sts, K2 tog, K1.
Continue dec in this way on every 4th row 2[2:3] times more, then on every alt row until 5 sts rem, ending with a P row. Leave sts on holder.

Neckband

Join raglan seams.
Using set of 4 No.9 needles and A, K left Back neck sts and left Sleeve sts, K up 9 sts down side of neck, K Front neck sts, K up 9 sts up other side of neck and K right Sleeve sts. 68[68:74] sts.
Continue in rounds of K1, P1 rib for 1½in. Cast off loosely in rib.

To make up

Press work lightly under a damp cloth, using a cool iron. Join side and sleeve seams. Fold neckband in half to inside and slip stitch in place. Press all seams.

Skirt back

Using No.7 needles and A, cast on 73[77:83] sts.
Work in rib as given for Back of Jumper for 4 rows, inc one st at end of last row. 74[78:84] sts.
Beg with a K row, continue in st st until work measures 8[8½:9]in from beg, or length required, ending with a P row and dec one st at end of last row.

Waistband

Change to No.9 needles.
Continue in rib as at beg for 10 rows. Cast off in rib.

Front

Work as for Back as far as waistband.

Waistband

Change to No.9 needles.
Continue in rib for 4 rows.
Next row Rib 13[14:14], cast off 2 sts, rib to last 15[16:16] sts, cast off 2 sts, rib to end.
Next row Rib to end casting on 2 sts over each 2 sts cast off.
Work 4 rows more in rib. Cast off in rib.

Straps

Using No.9 needles and A, cast on 11 sts.

Work in rib for 15½[16:17]in or length required.
Dec one st at each end of every row until 3 sts rem.
Break off yarn, thread through sts, draw up and fasten off.
Make a second strap in the same way.

To make up

Press work lightly under a damp cloth, using a cool iron. Join seams. Sew straight ends of straps to back waistband and sew button to other end of each strap.
Press all seams.

Trousers right leg

Using No.7 needles and A, cast on 71[73:75] sts and work in rib as on Back of Jumper for 4 rows, inc one st at end of last row. 72[74:76] sts.
Beg with a K row, continue in st st until work measures 13[14:15]in or length required, ending with a P row.

Shape crutch

Next row Cast off 4 sts, K to end.
Next row Cast off 6 sts, P to end.
Dec one st at each end of next and following 3 alt rows. 54[56:58] sts.
Continue straight until work measures 8[8½:9]in from beg of crutch shaping, or length required, ending with a P row and dec one st at end of last row.
Change to No.9 needles.
Continue in rib for 1in. Cast off in rib.

Left leg

Work to match right Leg, reversing all shaping.

To make up

Press work lightly under a damp cloth, using a cool iron. Join back and front seams. Join leg seams. Sew elastic to inside of waistband with casing. Press all seams.

Stitchery design / beading and embroidery stitches

Bead embroidery, rather more than any other form of the craft, lends itself to experimentation with unusual materials. All kinds of objects can be used as an embroidery decoration for clothes and furnishings, and this chapter gives some ideas for working with unusual things and combining them with beads and stitches.

Unusual materials

Besides beads and sequins, all kinds of things can be used to decorate fabrics, and many modern embroidery designers have produced quite striking pieces of work utilizing unlikely materials. Tap washers, curtain rings and trouser buttons, for instance, provide interesting round shapes, and there are dozens more to be found on ironmongers and haberdashery counters. Hooks and eyes, press studs, trouser fastenings, used in group and rows, look exciting and original. Bits of clock mechanism provide some unusually shaped pieces too, and lengths of plastic covered flex have been used with effective results. There are no fixed rules about what can or cannot be used in this kind of embroidery —anything goes, it's up to the embroiderer and her imagination.

Treatment of metal shapes

It may be necessary to varnish some metal objects before using them to prevent them rusting. Clear varnish is best for a protective covering but there is no reason why coloured nail varnish shouldn't be used for effect. Finish off with a coat of clear varnish seal to harden the nail polish off.

Beads combined with shapes

Many objects, such as tap washers, curtain rings and paper clips can be used individually to build up a design, but combined with beads they can look even more interesting. The trouser fastenings design illustrated in this chapter has been used in conjunction with beads, the beads used to secure the trouser fastening to the background fabric.

Sequin material

Sequin material can be cut with a pair of scissors into almost any shape and size to form giant sequin shapes. This is very useful because the large shapes provide a bold contrast to the smaller beads and sequins.

Sequin waste

This is the material from which the sequins have been cut, and it is full of sequin size holes. This sequin waste can be cut into lengths or an endless variety of shapes that

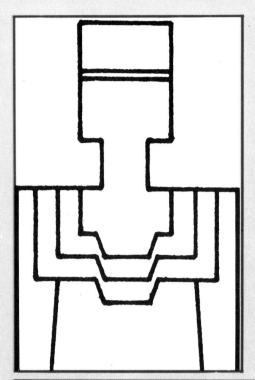

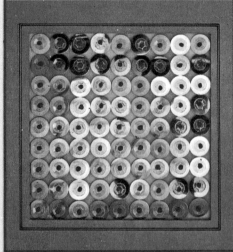

Left: stylised figure for bead embroidery
Above: formal arrangement of sequins
Below: trouser fastenings and beads arranged in rows to make a striking border design
Top right: contoured beads and sequins
Bottom right: beads and sequins in a hexagon
Far right: ways of using beads and stitches

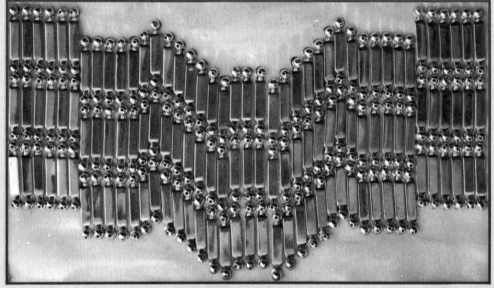

can be caught to the background fabric with embroidery stitches making use of the holes.

Rich borders can be formed with sequin waste by working rows of herringbone stitch or chain stitch in crewel wool. Lazy daisy stitch worked into six holes and either left as it is or finished off with a tiny bead in the centre looks interesting and is simple to do. Spider's web, also worked into six holes, gives a lovely contrast of texture.

Paillettes and mirrors

Paillettes have an attractive dull glow and combine well with bead embroidery. Mirrors have a brighter glitter and are cut by holding the mirror under water in a bowl, cutting it with a pair of old kitchen

scissors. One-sided handbag mirrors are ideal for this.

Beads combined with embroidery stitches

This is a most interesting technique with endless possibilities. Stitches such as herringbone, wheatear, stem, fly, feather and buttonhole look completely different when beads are actually worked into the stitches. Herringbone stitch, for example, looks interesting worked with large, oval, wooden beads or glass bugles, which in turn can be caught down at top and bottom with two or three small beads worked in a double back stitch. Lines of the design can be worked in beading broken up with intermittent areas of beading.

150

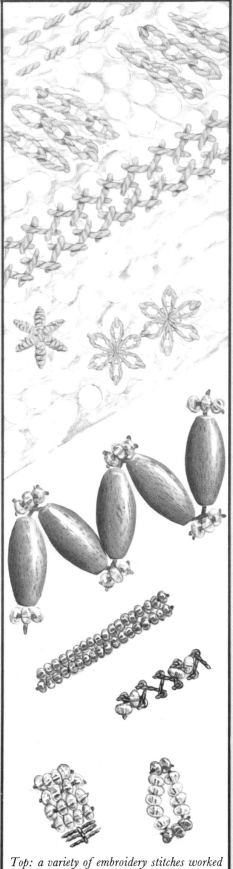

Top: a variety of embroidery stitches worked on sequin waste
Bottom: beads combined with embroidery stitches such as herringbone, Roumanian and coral knot

Stitchery pattern/rose-patterned slippers

A charming yellow rose design in canvas work for a pair of slippers. Work the pattern exactly the same for left and right foot; the instep shaping comes in the making up. The slippers can be made to fit any size foot by extending the tapered ends, but cut out the shape in paper before starting to check the fit of the upper.

For working a pair of slippers you will need:

☐ Double canvas, 10 holes to the inch, 26 inches by 13 inches
☐ Needlecord for lining half yard 36 inches wide
☐ Piece of leather 'split' or a piece of chamois for the soles
☐ One pair of cork soles to foot size
☐ Piece of stiff cardboard 12 inches by 12 inches
☐ Appleton's Crewel Wool. Three skeins 761 for the background, one skein each of the following: dull china blue range: 927, 925, 922; brown olive range: 313, 315; early English green range: 542, 544, 546; bright yellow: 552, 554; golden brown: 905; grey green: 352.
☐ Tapestry needle No.20
☐ Crewel needle No.7
☐ Embroidery frame

Working the design
Mark out the two slipper upper shapes on the canvas leaving space between them for making up. Mount the canvas in the frame. Mark the centre of each shape and work the design outwards.

Making up
Stretch the embroidery and cut out the uppers, leaving an inch of canvas all round. Using the cork insoles as a pattern cut out two more soles from the cardboard. Still using the cork insoles as a pattern, cut out the shape for each foot in the chamois and then in the needlecord fabric, leaving an extra inch all round. Cover the cardboard sole shapes with the chamois, lacing on the reverse side (see illustration). Cover the cork insoles with needlecord and lace in the same way.
Use the embroidered upper as a guide and cut out the needlecord linings and line the embroidered upper. Run a gathering thread $\frac{1}{8}$ inch in from the embroidery edging and drawing it up, try the uppers on, easing the gathers to fit the foot. Place the foot on the sole covered with needlecord and try the uppers again, turning the 1 inch of canvas to the underside of the insole. Pin and then stitch the uppers to the insole firmly. Glue the insole to the sole, wrong sides facing, using a fabric glue.

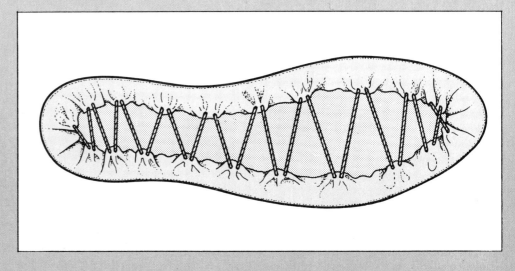

152

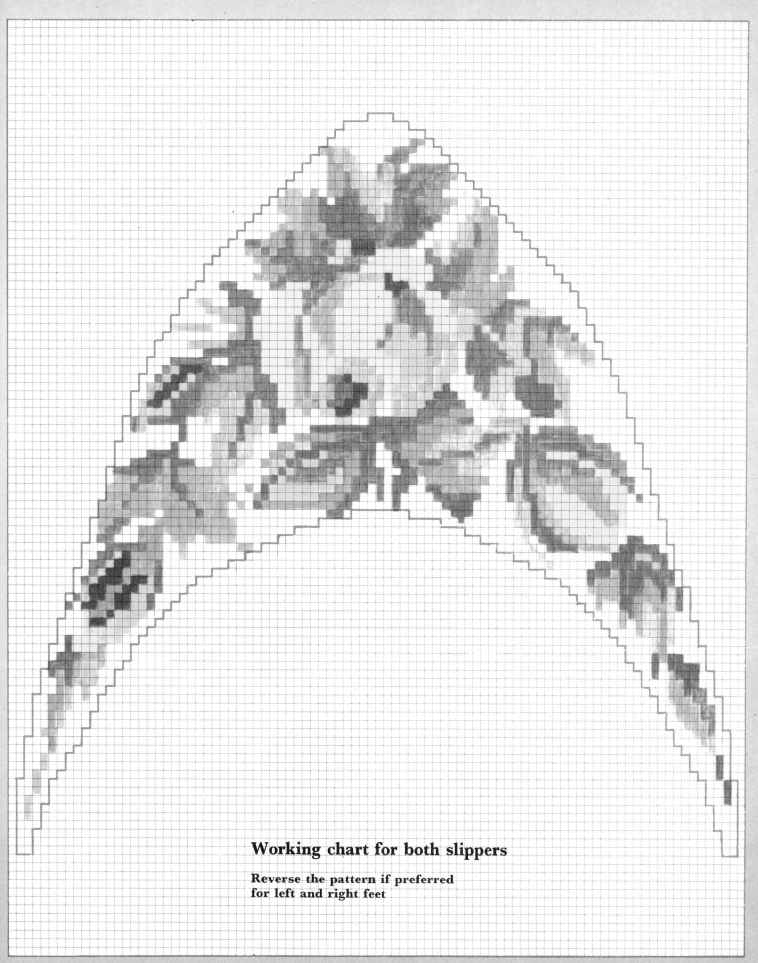

Working chart for both slippers

**Reverse the pattern if preferred
for left and right feet**

Home crochet/fireside rugs

The oval rug is worked from the centre and the round is worked in a long strip which is sewn up afterwards.

Fiery embers rug

Size
About 27in by 38in

> **Tension for this design**
> 5dc to 3in and 2 rows to 1in using double yarn worked with No. 7·00 hook

Materials shown here
Patons Turkey Rug Wool
1 skein poker red, A
3 skeins scarlet, B
4 skeins raspberry, C
5 skeins ruby, D
4 skeins black, E
One No.7·00 (ISR) crochet hook

Rug

Using No.7·00 hook and one strand each of A and B, make 18ch.
1st round 1dc into 2nd ch from hook, 1dc into each of next 15ch, 3dc into end ch, continue along other side of ch working 1dc into each of next 16 ch, 2dc into turning ch, ss into first st, turn.
2nd round 1ch, 1dc into same st, 2dc into each of next 2 sts, 1dc into each of next 16 sts, 2dc into each of next 3 sts, 1dc into each of next 16 sts, ss into 1ch, turn.
3rd round 1ch, 1dc into same st, 1dc into each of next 17 sts, (2dc into next st, 1dc into next st) 3 times, 1dc into each of next 16dc, (2dc into next st, 1dc into next st) twice, ss into 1ch, turn.
4th round 1ch, 1dc into same st, 1dc into each of next 2 sts, (2dc into next st, 1dc into each of next 2 sts) twice, 1dc into each of next 16 sts, (2dc into next st, 1dc into each of next

2 sts) 3 times, 1dc into each of next 16 sts, ss into 1ch.
Break off A.
Continue in this way into 3 sts at the curve on each round by placing one more st between inc on each round and keeping straight sides correct.
5th—7th rounds Work with 2 strands B.
8th—11th rounds Work with one strand each of B and C.
12th—14th rounds Work with 2 strands C.
15th—17th rounds Work with one strand each of C and D.
18th—20th rounds Work with 2 strands D.

154

21st—23rd rounds Work with one strand each of D and E.

24th—26th rounds Work with 2 strands E. Fasten off.

Spiral rag rug

Size
About 26in diameter plus fringe

Tension for this design
2dc to 1½in and 2 rows to 1in

Materials shown here
Tapis Pingouin
6 balls moutarde, A
2 balls tabac, B
1 ball rouge clair, C
1 ball imperiale, D
1 ball bleu franc, E
1 ball jonquille, F
One No.7·00 (ISR) crochet hook

Main section

Using No.7·00 hook and one strand each of A and B, make 3ch.

1st row 1dc into 2nd ch from hook, 1dc into next ch. 3 sts.

2nd row 1ch to count as first dc, 1dc into next dc, 1dc into turning ch.

Rep these 2 rows until work measures 10in.

Break off B and join in C, thus continuing with one strand each of A and C for a further 10in.

Continue in 10in sections, using yarn as follows:
A and E, A and F, A and D, A and B, A and C, A and E, A and F, A and D, A and B, A and D, A and C, A and E, A and F, A and C. A and E, A and B, (A and F, A and C, A and B, A and D) twice, A and E, A and C, A and F, A and D, A and B, A and E,

A and C, A and F, A and D, A and B, 36 sections. Fasten off.

To make up

Working on a flat surface, shape strip into a circle, overcasting on the wrong side with A and positioning colours as illustrated.

Fringe
Cut about 150 8in strands A and 75 8in strands B. Using 2 strands A and one strand B together throughout, knot into the edge of the rug at 1in intervals. Trim fringe.

Tailoring two

A. About basting

Always work on a flat surface when basting* seams, details and canvasses. This ensures that the grain is kept correctly aligned and not pulled out of shape.

Seams and details

1. Lay the pieces flat, right sides together, notches and balance marks matching exactly. Pin at right angles to the stitching line.
Using double thread baste together, starting with a tailor's knot* and finishing with a back stitch.

Seams with ease*

2a. Lay the pieces together, right sides facing, with the one to be eased on top. Pin the notches and divide ease equally along the length.
2b. Push ease down with fingers and baste, taking a small section at a time.

Back shoulder dart

In most cases it is better to ease in the back shoulder dart for a smoother line rather than stitch the dart. Exceptions are with linen, or fabric with a high man-made fibre content, because it is not easy to shrink these fibres.

Overbasting

3. Overbasting is used when basting for a fitting to give a smooth line and a better indication of fit.

B. The first fitting

Preparing for the first fitting

Before any sewing is done the coat must be basted together, tried on to see that it fits, and the initial alterations made.
4a. On the back, baste the style seams and baste the canvas to the wrong side along the neck and armholes.
4b. On the front, baste the style seams and the canvas darts or seams, then baste the
156

canvas to the wrong side.
Baste the sleeve seams.
4c. Baste the centre back seam of the under collar then baste the collar canvas to the wrong side of the under collar.
4d. Overbaste the side and shoulder seams and the under collar to the neck.
Baste the sleeves to the coat taking great care to spread the ease evenly at the sleeve head.

Fitting points

A well fitted coat feels comfortable, adjusts naturally to the activities of the wearer, is becoming in line and amount of ease, and is consistent with the current fashion.
Five interrelated factors are to be looked for when fitting a coat.
☐ Ease: there should be ease for movement without the coat being too large.
☐ Line: all vertical seams should be at right angles to the ground unless they are fashion features designed to be otherwise. All horizontal lines—the bust, waist, hips—should be at right angles to the vertical lines.
☐ Grain: as for line.
☐ Set or fit: a garment which sets well sits on the figure without wrinkles or strain.
☐ Balance: pockets, belts, buttons, hems to be proportioned correctly for the individual figure.

Correcting the faults

Put on the coat, right side out, over the appropriate clothing. Pin the centre front lines together and then check the following points. It is better if you can get a friend to help you here.
☐ Is the coat sitting on the figure correctly (**5**)? Are the lower edges level, the centre back and centre front lines vertical?
☐ Are the style lines right for the figure—sometimes a line over the bust can be moved for better balance (**6**).
☐ Look for strain points shown by wrinkles (**7a**). Unbaste and let seams out till wrinkles have gone. Repin.
☐ If the coat is too big it will hang in folds (**7b**). Unbaste and repin.
☐ Turn up the hem and check buttonhole and pocket positions. Unless they are fashion features, pockets should be placed so that they are easy to use—the usual position is about 2 inches below the waist and between the centre front and side seam. If your hip or stomach is rather large a pocket could be inserted in a seam to give a smoother line (see Golden Hands chapter 39).
☐ Check that the fold of the lapel is lying smoothly and continues on the undercollar (**8a, b**). An adjustment to the top button

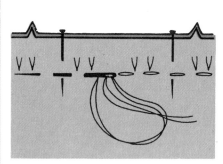

1. *Basting a straight seam*

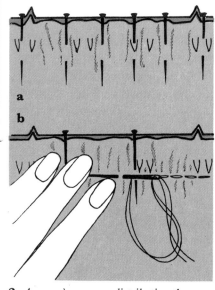

2. *An eased seam:* **a.** *distributing the ease;* **b.** *pushing in the ease and basting*

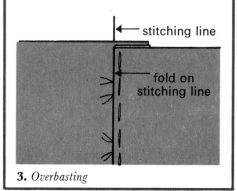

3. *Overbasting*

position can correct a loose or tight neck line (**8c**). An adjustment at the back neck seam may be necessary for a shawl collar to sit well.
Pin along the folds and thread mark when unbasted (**8a, b**).
☐ See that the sleeve hangs smoothly, that it is not too large or tight, and that the armhole line is well balanced. However, no alterations to the sleeve are made at this stage; the sleeves are put in to check the appearance and balance of the coat.

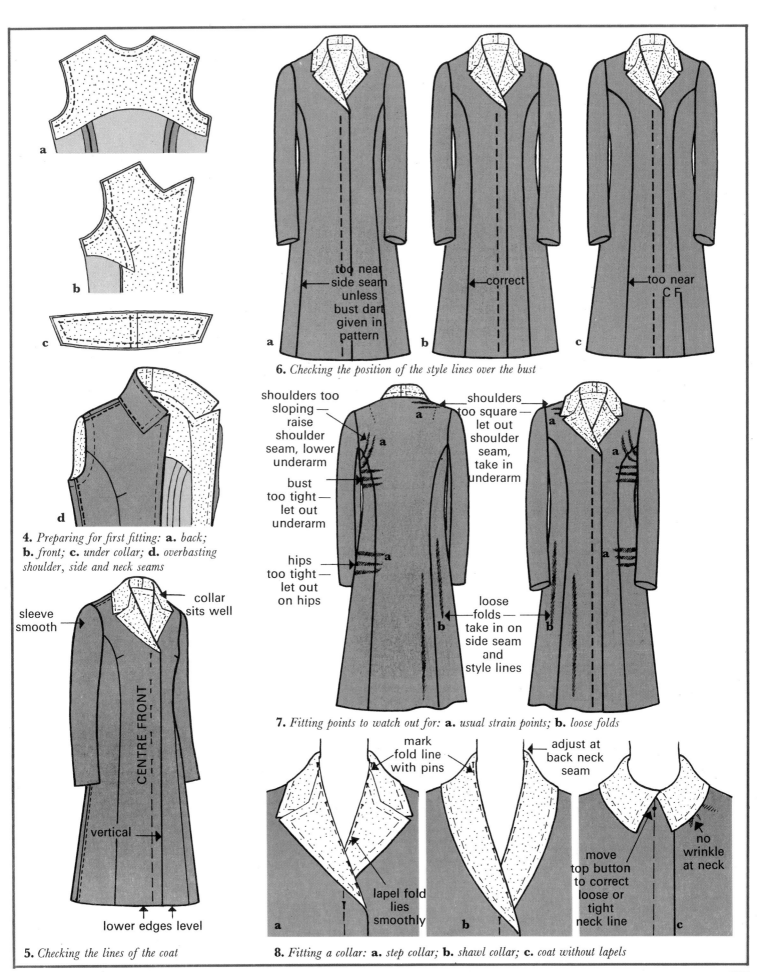

a

b

c

d

4. *Preparing for first fitting:* **a.** *back;* **b.** *front;* **c.** *under collar;* **d.** *overbasting shoulder, side and neck seams*

collar sits well

sleeve smooth

CENTRE FRONT

vertical

lower edges level

5. *Checking the lines of the coat*

too near side seam unless bust dart given in pattern

a

correct

b

too near C F

c

6. *Checking the position of the style lines over the bust*

shoulders too sloping — raise shoulder seam, lower underarm

bust too tight — let out underarm

hips too tight — let out on hips

a

a

a

shoulders too square — let out shoulder seam, take in underarm

a

a

loose folds — take in on side seam and style lines

b

b

7. *Fitting points to watch out for:* **a.** *usual strain points;* **b.** *loose folds*

mark fold line with pins

lapel fold lies smoothly

a

b

adjust at back neck seam

move top button to correct loose or tight neck line

no wrinkle at neck

c

8. *Fitting a collar:* **a.** *step collar;* **b.** *shawl collar;* **c.** *coat without lapels*

Pinning alterations

9a, b. To let out or take in a seam, first unbaste. Find the correct position for the seam then fold one side on the new stitching line and pin fold to new stitching line on under piece.

Marking alterations

10. On shoulders and side seams thread mark any alterations in a new coloured thread.

Mark through the fold and along the under piece.

Remove old markings.

11. On style seams slip baste* any alterations through fold and under piece. Remove old markings.

Preparing to stitch

Unbaste sleeve, under collar, shoulder and side seams, but leave the style seams basted.

C. About stitching

Seams

12. To avoid damage to the fabric remove the tailor's tacks before machining and then stitch just outside the line of basting without catching it.

Seams with ease should be stitched with the ease side up as they are easier to control this way.

Shoulder seams

13. Shoulder seams, however, are best hand sewn. For a firm result use a double silk thread and a back stitch. By doing this the ease is controlled, resulting in a straight line.

14. Before a seam is pressed the basting is removed and the edges neatened by overcasting in matching silk thread.

Topstitching

Topstitching gives a professional finish when done carefully, so practise on a piece of fabric folded to the appropriate thickness.

Work the topstitching as the garment is being made, not when it is finished.

For topstitching work as follows:

☐ Set the machine to a large stitch.
☐ Use a number 16 (or 100) needle.
☐ If possible use buttonhole twist in both bottom and top of the machine. If you find this does not work try threading the top only.
☐ Check bobbin and refill if low.
☐ Baste just inside the topstitching line (**15**). Then stitch slowly and carefully, using basting, seam and machine foot as guide lines. When turning corners leave the needle in the work and pivot cloth on needle.

158

D. Pressing

To ensure a smoothly finished garment each stage of the work should be pressed as it is finished. This needs care and plenty of patience.

Remember that pressing is not ironing and that the iron should be lifted and pressed upon the part required—not smoothed to and fro.

16. The positioning of the garment or part to be pressed is important and you should work in the direction of the grain.

Always test for the correct iron temperature on a spare piece of fabric. If there are any artificial fibres in the cloth regulate the heat to these to avoid destroying them.

Using a tailor's clapper

Pressing cloths must be damp rather than wet to avoid spoiling the appearance of the fabric and leaving a rough-dry look.

17. As the iron is lifted after each pressing, quickly remove the damp cloth and hold the tailor's clapper firmly over the pressed section for some seconds. This action helps to set the seam or edge professionally, ensuring a crisper fold or flatter surface.

Press and clap the folds of pleats, hems, seams, darts, pockets and edges as the construction of the garment proceeds.

Pressing seams

18. Remove all basting and press the seam flat to blend the stitches.

19. Lay the seam over a pressing roll, making sure that the rest of the garment is well supported. Press open with the point of the iron as shown.

20. Look at the right side to make sure the seam line is flat before pressing with a damp cloth and clapping heavily on the wrong side.

Pressing eased seams

Where a seam has been eased or fabric is to be moulded the technique of shrinking* is used.

21. Lay the garment flat on an ironing board, right side down. Shrink away the ease with the point of the iron and a damp pressing cloth.

22. Open the seam, lay over a pressing roll and shrink the eased seam edge. While damp stretch * the uneased edge.

Finally press and clap the seam.

Pressing darts

23a. After stitching, cut along the fold of the dart, cutting as near to the point as possible.

23b. Lay the dart right side down over a ham and press and clap the dart open, checking for a smooth line.

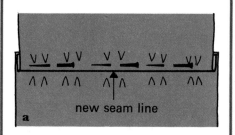

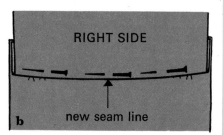

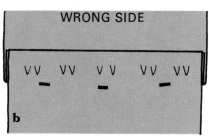

9a, b. *Letting out and taking in a seam*

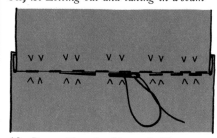

10. *Re-marking shoulder and side seams*

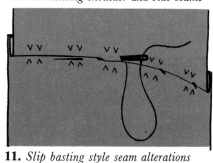

11. *Slip basting style seam alterations*

Top pressing

Top pressing is used for lapels, collars and the final press.

Lay the garment on an ironing board right side up, smoothed into the correct position with the grain undistorted.

Cover with a piece of light-weight wool cloth. Over this place the pressing cloth and press lightly. This prevents shine and removes any pin, basting or seam marks which might have been accidentally pressed in.

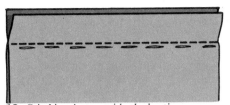

12. *Stitching just outside the basting*

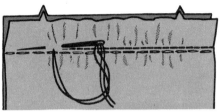

13. *Backstitching an eased shoulder seam*

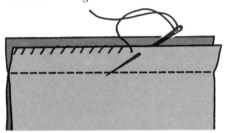

14. *Overcasting the seam edges*

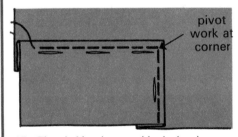

pivot
work at
corner

15. *Topstitching just outside the basting*

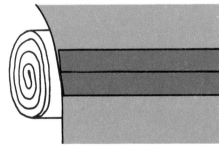

16. *Pressing a carefully positioned seam*

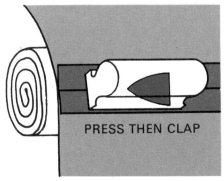

PRESS THEN CLAP

17. *Using a tailor's clapper*

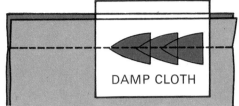

DAMP CLOTH

18. *A seam pressed flat*

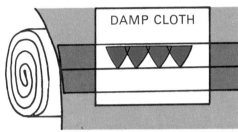

DAMP CLOTH

19. *Pressing a seam open with point of iron*

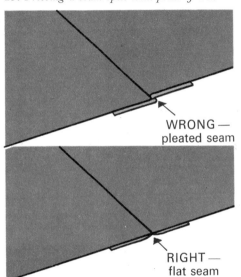

WRONG —
pleated seam

RIGHT —
flat seam

20. *Checking that seam is flat before clapping*

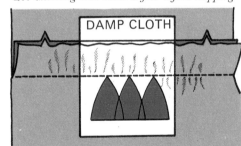

DAMP CLOTH

21. *Shrinking ease in a seam*

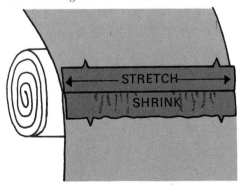

STRETCH

SHRINK

22. *Pressing the eased seam open*

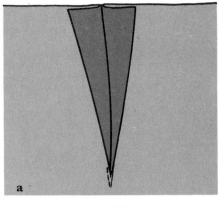

a

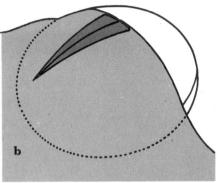

b

23. *Cutting a dart open;* **b.** *positioning open dart over a tailor's ham*
Butterick pattern 6528, made up in cashmere, shows decorative topstitching

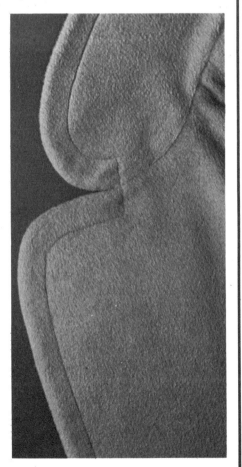

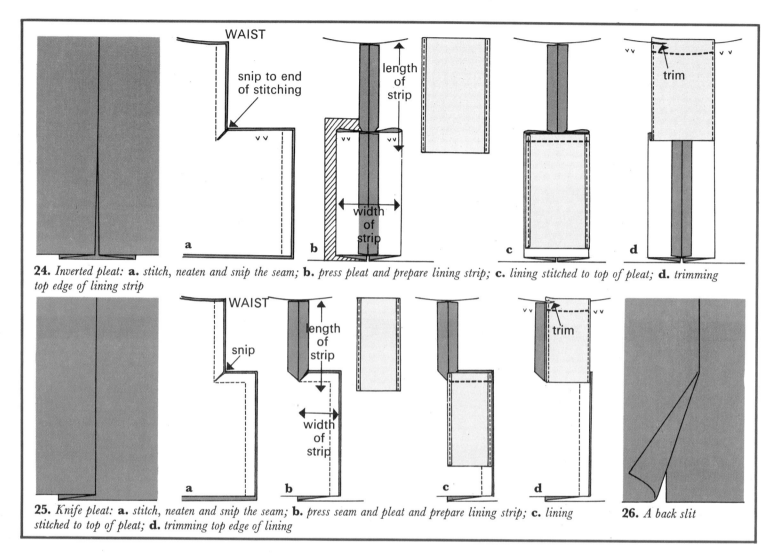

24. *Inverted pleat:* **a.** *stitch, neaten and snip the seam;* **b.** *press pleat and prepare lining strip;* **c.** *lining stitched to top of pleat;* **d.** *trimming top edge of lining strip*

25. *Knife pleat:* **a.** *stitch, neaten and snip the seam;* **b.** *press seam and pleat and prepare lining strip;* **c.** *lining stitched to top of pleat;* **d.** *trimming top edge of lining*   26. *A back slit*

E. Pleats

Because of the heavier fabrics used in tailoring all pleats need to be supported to prevent them dragging and upsetting the balance of the garment.

Inverted pleat
24a. Baste, fit, stitch, snip and neaten the seams. Press open.

24b. Put seams in line and press pleat, placing brown paper or card under the fold to prevent marking the fabric.
Cut a strip of lining to the pleat width plus $\frac{1}{2}$ inch, and to the length from the top stitching line of the pleat to the neck or waist.
Turn under each long edge for $\frac{1}{4}$ inch and stitch.

24c. Stitch this strip to each fold of the pleat.

24d. Fold up and stitch it to the coat just above the neck or waist seam. Trim to the curve.

Knife pleat
25a. Baste, fit, stitch, snip and neaten seams.

25b. Press the coat seam open and the pleat seam flat. Cut a strip of lining fabric to the pleat width plus $\frac{1}{2}$ inch, and to the length from top stitching line of slit to the neck or waist. Turn under the long edges for $\frac{1}{4}$ inch and stitch.

25c. Stitch this strip to the top of the pleat.

25d. Fold up and stitch it to the coat just above the neck or waist seam. Trim to the curve.

Slit opening (26)
Stitch as given for the slit opening in the pattern, then support as for knife pleat.

*Terms and stitches

Basting: firm tacking with $\frac{1}{4}$ inch stitches.
Easing: instead of a dart, shaping is obtained by easing one seam to another.
Shrinking: to shrink away the extra fullness which gives ease and to create shaping.
Slip basting (27): used to baste a seam from the right side after altering a seam (also used to match patterns, plaids, stripes etc). Fold top piece under on sewing line. Place fold over sewing line of lower piece. Sew taking a $\frac{1}{2}$ inch stitch

through fold then a $\frac{1}{2}$ inch stitch through under piece along the sewing line.

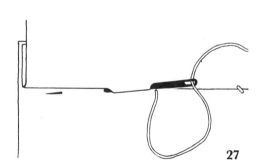

27

Stretching: to stretch fabric to make it lie flat as in curved seams, and to create shaping.
Tailor's knot (28):

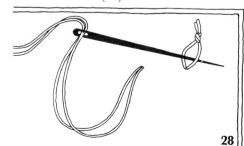

28

160

Crafts/candlemaking

Original candles

Using quite simple equipment and a lot of imagination, an almost infinite variety of candle shapes can be made. Some of the ideas in this chapter are beautiful and some are astonishing — such as the water candles above.

Materials and equipment
Assemble the materials before starting work. A candlemakers supplier will stock most of them.

You will need:
- [ ] Paraffin wax
- [ ] Beeswax sheets (for beeswax candles)
- [ ] Stearin
- [ ] Wax dyes
- [ ] Candle perfumes (if perfumed candles are required)
- [ ] Wicks
- [ ] Sugar thermometer
- [ ] Two large saucepans: one is for melting wax, the other for dissolving colour
- [ ] Enamel jug with a lip for pouring molten wax
- [ ] Deep enamel jug for making dipped candles
- [ ] Mould seal (plasticine or clay)
- [ ] Ruler
- [ ] Wicking needle (to make holes for wicks)
- [ ] Deep receptacle for cold water
- [ ] Moulds
- [ ] Spoons for ladling molten wax
- [ ] Sand, for sand casting, in a box

Paraffin wax. The types of paraffin wax available vary widely, but is recommended that a fully refined wax with a melting point of 135°-140°F be used. This type of paraffin wax is available from candlemakers suppliers in solid blocks or in a powdered form, which may be more convenient.

Wicks. Candlewicks are made of bleached linen thread and these are woven and graded to burn a certain area of wax. Wicks are usually sold in packs and sized according to the diameter of the candle they will successfully burn. A 1 inch wick will burn a candle 1 inch in diameter, and it will also burn a 1 inch hole in a larger candle. It is therefore essential to use the correct size of wick; a large candle with a small wick looks very nice when burning—until the wick drowns in a pool of wax.

Wax dyes. Candles can be left white or coloured with dye—wax dyes are the best for the job. These are available in either powder or solid form. It is advisable to test dyes carefully, as too much dye will diminish the candle's glow. Test by taking a spoonful of the coloured candle wax and putting it in cold water. As it sets you will get an idea of the final shade. For most colours a tiny pinch of powdered dye will colour a pint of liquid wax.

Stearin. Dye is dissolved first in stearin— a white, flaky type of wax which allows the dye to dissolve readily and completely with perfect colour suspension. The proportion added is 10 per cent stearin to wax.

Thermometer. A sugar thermometer with readings up to a temperature of 400°F must be used, for although there is little danger of over-heating the wax to the point where it will burst into flames it is

161

impossible to judge when the wax is at the correct temperature, and it is the temperature at which the wax is worked which gives many of the different effects.

Moulds. Although craft shops sell ready-made moulds of rubber, glass and metal, improvised moulds work very well and can produce fascinating shapes. Some household containers can be used, as long as they are leakproof and do not collapse under the heat of the wax. Yoghurt cartons, tins, cardboard cartons, plastic drainpipe, rubber balls, balloons, acetate and PVC sheeting are some of the things which can be utilized for moulds, but remember that the candle has to be removed when it has set, therefore the mould must either have a wide neck or be breakable.

Preparing the wax for coloured candles

Measure out the powdered wax or break up block wax into pieces. Measure out the stearin, one part stearin to ten parts of wax. Melt the stearin in a saucepan and then add the dye. Stir until all the particles of dye are dissolved. Melt the paraffin wax slowly in the second saucepan and then add the stearin and dye mixture.

White candles can be covered with a final layer of colour by dipping them into molten coloured wax. Float a 2 inch layer of molten coloured wax · on hot water (heated at 82°C 180°F). Dip the white candle through the wax and into the water, then withdraw it so that it picks up colour along its length. If the wax is too hot very little colour will be picked up, and conversely, if the wax is too cool, the colour will be flaky. This dipping process can be repeated for depth of colour.

Candlemaking methods

Dipping

Dipping is one of the oldest methods of candlemaking and all that is required is wick, wax and an enamel jug, a little deeper than the required length of candle. Attach a piece of wick to a small stick. Fill the jug with wax heated at 82°C, 180°F. Dip the wick into the wax. Remove it and hold it in the air for about half a minute, or until the coat of wax has hardened. Dip again and repeat until the candle is thick enough. As the wax in the jug cools, bubbles will appear on the surface of the wax or the candle. When this happens, reheat the wax to 180°F. When the candle is finished, hang it to harden. For an all white candle or for one coloured throughout a good finishing shine can be given by giving a final dip

162

▲ *Statue-made mould* ▼ *Rolled beeswax sheets*

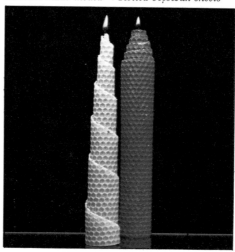

in wax heated to 200°F, 93°C, and then plunging the candle into cold water. If the jug is wide enough at the neck, several candles can be made by dipping simultaneously.

Ways with dipped candles

Moulding dipped candles

Candles can be moulded to shape by hand between dips. The pear shaped candles illustrated were made in this way.
Build up the candle to about ½ inch diameter, then start to dip or pour wax from half way up; the lower part of the candle will begin to thicken. At this stage, between dips, roll the candle between the hands towards the shape you want.

Carved candles

By dipping a short length of wick in a succession of different colours, building them up to about ¼ inch thick, multi-coloured layers are formed and these can be carved back with a sharp knife to great effect. For this process the wax must be very strongly dyed, or the layers of colour will show through each other.

▲ *Ready made mould* ▼ *Carved dipped candle*

To save wax follow the method given for floating coloured wax on hot water, but make a centre core of at least 1 inch thickness by the normal dipping method first to prevent water getting on the wick.

Twist and plaits

A plait of three dipped candles in contrasting colours looks effective and these are easily made if someone else holds the ends while one plaits. A twisted candle is made with a finished but still soft dipped candle. Lay it on a smooth clean surface and flatten it gently with a rolling pin. Square off the base and, taking the candle in both hands, twist top and bottom in opposite directions. Cool immediately in cold water.

Beeswax candles

Sheets of pure beeswax, honeycomb textured and smelling delightfully of honey, can be used to make simple candles. These sheets are available from candlemakers suppliers. Choose a suitable wick and cut it to the desired candle length plus a few more inches. Lay the wick along one edge of the sheet and fold the wax over to cover

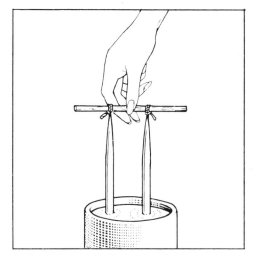

▲ *The technique of dipping candles*
▼ *The technique for layered candles*

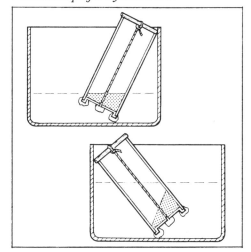

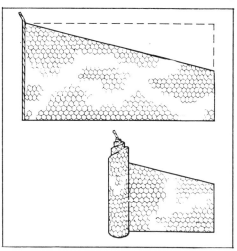

▲ *Beeswax sheet cut for rolling*
▼ *Candle mould suspended and filled*

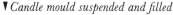

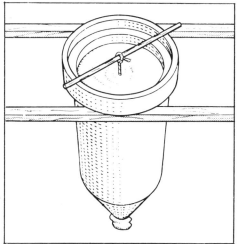

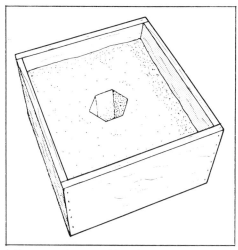

▲ *Damp sand prepared in a box*
▼ *The sand mould before carving*

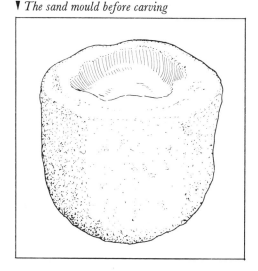

it. Roll up the candle, gently and evenly, making sure that the base is level. Trim the wick and dip it in molten beeswax. To make a pointed candle, cut the sheet of beeswax as shown in the diagram. Two contrasting tints of beeswax sheeting can be used together for variation.

Moulded candles

Ready-made moulds

Craft shops sell different kinds of ready-made candle moulds made of both metal and flexible latex rubber. Decorative relief candles are made in these in one casting. Treat latex rubber moulds with care, washing and drying them carefully after use. These moulds have no wick holes, and this has to be made with a wick needle. Make sure that the same hole is used each time the mould is used. To wick-up a mould thread the wick through, tying the bottom end to a rod or a stick with the top end of the wick pulled tight. Seal the hole with mould seal. Support the mould by hanging it on an improvised rack (see diagram).

To make a candle heat the wax to 180°F

and pour it slowly into the mould. Tap the sides of the mould gently to release air bubbles. After a short while a well will form round the wick as the cooling wax contracts. Prod the surface to break it and top up with wax heated to 180°F. Do this as often as necessary until the surface of the candle remains flat. If the candle seems to be misshapen, manipulate the mould with the hands while it is still soft. When the candle is completely cold and hardened rub the surface of the mould with soapy hands, and peel back the mould, taking care around the wick area. Return the mould to its original shape, wash and dry it. Remove the wick rod from the candle and trim the base.

The candle surface can be polished with hands or a soft cloth. Add a small amount of beeswax to the paraffin wax for a better shine.

Relief work can be highlighted by colouring the surface of the candle with water—soluble paint mixed with a little soap. Paint the candle and rub the colour off just before it dries, leaving some in the crevices. Do not over-do the colour because water soluble paint does not burn, and

may clog the wick if used to excess.

Making flexible moulds

Mould for making candles are made from a moulding liquid which is obtained from candle makers suppliers. Choose an ornament, jar or statue made from wood, glass, plastic, stone, plaster or clay. Make sure it is free from dust or grease.

Heat the object gently in front of a fire and dip it into the moulding liquid, covering it completely. Remove and hold the object until it stops dripping. The mould will set faster with a little heat, so hold the object in front of a fan heater until the whitish colour changes to yellow. The first few dips will go almost transparent. Air bubbles must be blown off and care must be taken not to touch the setting mould. Continue to dip until a smooth, even coat of about one sixteenth of an inch thick or more has built up. Leave the mould to stand until the moulding material has set. Trim uneven edges, and after rubbing the surface with liquid soap peel it away. Make a wick hole at the top of the mould and use it in exactly the same way as ready-made flexible moulds.

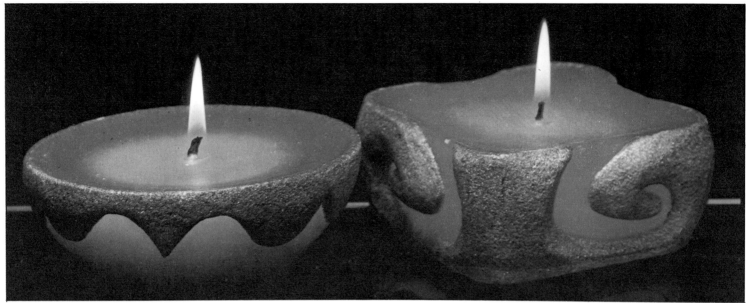

▲ Sand candles from an ashtray and bowl—carved into castles ▼ *▼ Two candles using the chunk technique. The square was made in a tea tin*

Other candlemaking techniques

Sand candles. Fill a box with damp sand and smooth off the surface without packing it down. Dig a hole out of the centre and push an article into the hole to make a shaped hole.

An ashtray, small bowl or the end of a bottle will do. Heat the wax to 250°F, and pour it into shape in the sand, taking care to pour into the centre of the hole. The hotter the wax, the more sand is picked up; at 250°F, between ½ inch and 1 inch is picked up. If a thicker sand wall is required, the wax should be hotter. Refill the hole as the level of the wax falls, keeping the temperature

164

of the wax high. Allow the sand candle to harden in a cold place for 1-2 hours. After this time, push the wicking needle down the centre and leave it standing upright. Leave the candle overnight. Next day, dig the candle out, loosening the sand around it carefully and brushing away loose sand. Remove the needle and insert a wick which will leave an inch of wax unburned (for instance, if the candle is 3 inches in diameter put a 2 inch wick in). Top up with melted wax (220°F) and allow to set. Carve away areas of sand to make a design, taking care not to dig too deeply into the wax. If the right wick is chosen, the sand shell will remain intact after the candle has burned out and can be refilled.

Chunky candles. Arrange chunks of coloured wax in a mould, pressing them to the sides and keeping them as far apart as possible. Pour molten wax (200°F) over these chunks. Allow the mould to stand for one minute, then place in a cooling bath. Push a wicking needle down the centre. When set, take the mould from the bath, and place it in water just under boiling point. The outside of the wax will melt, and the coloured chunks will also melt and blend with the new wax. Top up with wax at 180°F, covering the whole surface of the candle and allowing the wax to flow down the inside of the mould so that the whole surface is covered with molten wax. Place mould in a cooling bath again and allow to harden. Remove

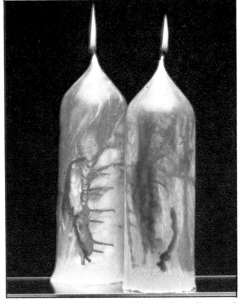

▲▼ Marbled effects on multilayered candles, and two from a ball and a balloon ▲

▲▼ Beeswax candles and water candles

candle, put in wick.

Marbled candles. Fix a wick in a warmed solid mould, and pour in a wax-stearin mixture at 190°F. Allow a minute for air bubbles to rise, then place in a cooling ·bath for 40 seconds. Pour the unset wax back into the pan, leaving a wax shell in the mould. Then, using pure dye, spoon a little into the mould, and quickly swirl it round and tip away the excess. Do this two or three times· with different colours until a design has built up. Then pour in half a cup of candle wax (180°F), swirl it round quickly and empty the excess into a separate container (so that the wax will not contaminate white wax if it has picked up colour). Do this seven or eight times to trap the colour between

two layers of white wax. Then fill the mould with candle wax in the usual way. To achieve a well defined pattern it is essential that the mould is kept warm and that there is no waiting between processes.

Multi-layered candles. These are made by pouring different coloured waxes into a mould at 82°F, allowing each layer to partially set before adding the next colour. By standing the mould at an angle in a cooling bath, layers can be built up diagonally.

Ball candles. Round candles are made using a rubber ball as a mould. Cut the ball in half and cut a hole in the top. Stick the two halves together again with sticky tape.

Whipped cream candles. Whip cooling

wax with a fork to make a frothy mixture and use it to make candles in moulds which wouldn't stand higher temperatures.

Water candles. These strange looking candles are intended to be used for table decorations but they can be burned. Put a small quantity of melted wax (210°F) into a saucer and, wearing rubber gloves, hold a plain candle upright, resting in the wax. Holding the saucer in one hand and the candle in the other, push the candle and saucer into a bucket of cold water with a swift, smooth movement. The wax will float upwards, and practice will gradually make the formation less random. By twisting the saucer as it is immersed, the wax can be swirled around the candle.

Knitting design/working without patterns

A problem facing owners of home knitting machines is the comparative scarcity of knitting patterns. Hand knitting patterns are mostly produced by the yarn spinners themselves and a tremendous number are printed each year. The majority of machine knitting instructions, however, are prepared by the manufacturers—each design planned to work on that company's machine alone. This situation imposes a certain limitation on the knitting machine owner, who is not always able to find exactly the garment pattern she requires and in the right size. These chapters are planned to help the machine knitter to get the best out of her machine by learning to work without commercially printed patterns. The simplest things to make are those formed from long strips of knitting—home furnishings, for instance.

Experimenting with yarns and stitches
Once a home knitting machine owner has become completely familiar with the working of her machine and has successfully made a few garments, she will look around for ideas about other things to make. The speed of working and the constant evenness of stitch which is achieved on modern knitting machines means that quite large areas of knitted fabric can be considered and this factor opens up a whole new world of things to knit.

To a certain extent, it depends on the knitting machine as to the range of fabrics and garments that can be produced upon it. Some machines are limited to using 4 ply yarns and very simple stitch patterns. Other machines are designed to use a wider range of yarns, from a fine nylon spun to chunky triple knits, and will work them into Fair Isle patterns, knit-weave fabrics or dainty lace fabrics.

Whatever the model of machine and whatever its performance, it is up to the user to experiment with different types of yarns and stitch combinations until she knows exactly what her machine is capable of producing. The manufacturer's handbook, supplied with your machine, will tell you that hundreds of different patterns are possible, and many of them will be illustrated. Machine knitting, however, has only lately begun to be developed as a new and exciting craft medium, and part of the enjoyment of owning a machine lies in experimenting with combinations of yarns and stitches to create your own wonderful and completely original fabrics. Buy single balls of yarn and make up square swatches, trying out every stitch combination of which your machine is capable. Note the yarn gauge, the tension dial number and your working procedure

and label each swatch. You'll find these invaluable as a reference when you begin to design your own garments.

Designing on a knitting machine
Much of what has been written in the previous Knitting Design chapters applies to designing for machine knitting. Read these chapters again and refresh your know-how for taking body measurements and charting. One of the greatest differences however, is the fact that one must calculate the number of rows to the inch and number of stitches to the inch exactly from a swatch before starting, because it is practically impossible to take any measurements from the work once it is stretched on the machine.

The greatest care must be taken in making a tension swatch. This must be worked to at least four inches by four inches, larger if possible. Steam and press the swatch without stretching, so that it resembles the texture of the finished garment, and then measure it, following the method described in Golden Hands Knitting Know-how Chapter 1. You will find that the finished garment will work out at the same number of stitches to the inch and will fit exactly just as you planned. In general, the method for planning the shape of garment pieces and working with measurements and charts as described in the previous chapters will work equally well for machine knitting. It is of course important that the knitter is completely familiar with, and has mastered, the basic methods of operating her machine, and can increase and decrease, make darts and flares and shape simple pieces according to the instructions given in the machine handbook.

Other ways of shaping pieces of knitted fabric to make garments, and some of the knitting machine manufacturers aids which are available, are covered in later chapters.

Simple things to make without patterns
The easiest thing to knit on a knitting machine is, of course, a long and wide strip of fabric. Depending on the kind of machine you own, this fabric can be lacy, chunkily woven, finely textured or knit-woven, it can look like tweed or like folk weave, it can be striped, spotted or chequered, have bands of coloured pattern, have single large motifs or a small all over pattern.

Different machines have widely varying pattern possibilities, and if you have experimented sufficiently you will know what your particular machine can achieve. The fabric you knit, in your own particular choice of colour and stitch, will be an

exclusive fabric, suitable not only for garments but for making home furnishings.

Knitting for the home
Knitted furnishing fabric has the advantage of being both hardwearing and elastic and can therefore be made to fit chairs, seat cushions, divans etc, extremely well. Curtains and bedcovers knitted in a fine yarn using a lacy pattern not only hang well but they can be worked to match a colour scheme or fitted to an awkwardly shaped window with very little difficulty. In the room setting illustrated, the lacy curtains and bedcover were knitted using a punch card pattern on a Knitmaster 321. Both were worked without shaping, and the bedspread has a piped-edged frill, also worked on the machine.

In the next chapter more furnishing ideas are given where the fabrics have been produced on a home knitting machine. There is a charming bedspread and curtains to match, linked by a giraffe motif which uses two punch cards joined together. As a contrast, the sitting room setting, in cream and brown tones, uses different punch card patterns and knitting techniques, including knit-weaving.

This pretty room setting uses machine knitted lace fabric for both the curtains and the bedspread. They were knitted on a Knitmaster punch card machine, model 321, using Robin Tricel/Nylon Perle, together with a transparent thread, to produce the lace effect ►
Detail of the fabric ▼

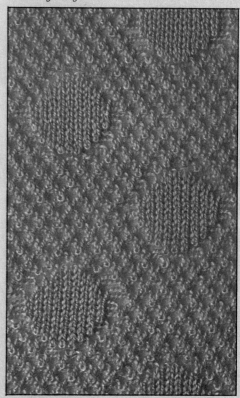

Knitting pattern/chunky jacket

The fastest thing on two pins is just the way to describe this long line cardigan. Worked on very large needles and using three strands of yarn simultaneously, it's fun to work and quick to complete. The result is a warm, richly textured cover-up to go with casual outfits when the temperature drops. A purchased belt is optional.

Sizes

To fit 34[36:38:40]in bust loosely
Length, 31[31:32½:32½]in
Sleeve seam, 15½[16:16½:17]in

> **Tension for this design**
> 6 sts and 9 rows to 4in over st st worked on ¾in maxi pins using 3 strands yarn

Materials shown here

Wendy Diabolo Double Double Knit Nylonised 20[23:23:23] 50 grm balls
One pair ¾in maxi pins
4 buttons

Back

Using 3 strands yarn tog throughout, with ¾in maxi pins cast on 31[31:33:33] sts.
1st row K1, *P1, K1, rep from * to end.
2nd row P1, *K1, P1, rep from * to end.
Beg with a K row, continue in st st until work measures 8[8:9:9]in, ending with a P row.
K2 tog at each end of the next and following 6th row.
Continue without shaping until work measures 23[23:24 24]in from beg, ending with a P row.

Shape armholes

K2 tog at each end of next and every alt row until 9 sts rem, ending with a P row. Cast off.

Left front

Cast on 15[17:17:19] sts.
Work 2 rows in rib as given for Back, inc one st at end of last row. 16[18:18:20] sts.
168

Next row K5[6:6:7], K into second st on left hand needle then K first st on left hand needle and slip both sts off tog—called TW2R —, placing needle behind first st on left hand needle K into back of second st then K first st and slip both sts off tog—called TW2L —, K to end.
Next row K2, P to end.
Rep the last 2 rows until work measures 11½[12:12:12½]in, ending with a WS row.
Next row K3[4:4:5], (P1, K1) twice, M1P, (K1, P1) twice, K to end.
Next row K2, P3[4:4:5], K1, (P1, K1) 4 times, P to end.
Next row K3[4:4:5], cast off 9 sts in rib, K to end.
With a separate length of yarn and a spare needle, cast on 8 sts. Work 3 rows st st thus ending with a K row. Break off yarn.
Return to where main piece of work was left.
Next row K2, P3[4:4:5], P the 8 sts on spare needle, P to end.
Keeping the centre 4 sts in patt as before, continue without shaping until work measures the same as Back to armholes, ending with a WS row.

Shape armhole and front edge

Next row K2 tog, patt to last 4 sts, K2 tog, K2.
Continue dec in this way at front edge on every alt row 4[6:5:7] times more, *at the same time* dec at armhole edge on every alt row until 2 sts rem.
Continue on these 2 sts in g st for 5in. Cast off.

Right front

Work to match left Front, reversing all shaping.

Sleeves

Cast on 13[13:15:15] sts.
Work 2 rows in rib as on Back, inc one st in centre of last row. 14[14:16:16] sts.
Next row K5[5:6:6], TW2R, TW2L, K to end.
Next row P to end.

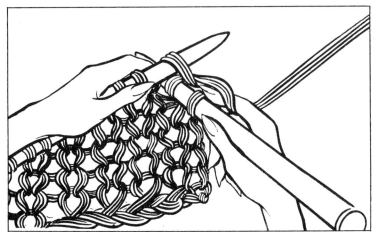

▲ *Showing the scale of the maxi-pins*
▼ *Close-up detail of TW2R which forms the cable-like panel*

Keeping patt correct in centre, inc one st at each end of every 5th row until there are 22[22: 26:26] sts.
Continue without shaping until sleeve seam measures 15½[16:16½:17]in, ending with a P row.

Shape top

K2 tog at each end of next and every alt row until 4[4:6:6] sts rem, ending with a P row.

Cast off.

To make up

Press work lightly under a damp cloth using a warm iron. Join raglan seams. Join side and sleeve seams. Join ends of Front bands and sew to Back neck. Make pocket linings from fabric and stitch in place. Sew on buttons using holes in knitting for buttonholes. Press seams.

Stitchery design/candlewicking

Candlewick originated in America in early Colonial days when, with a severe shortage of sewing materials of all kinds, women settlers used the thick cotton wick intended for candlemaking as an embroidery thread, working it into knotted and tufted designs on bedspreads. For many years the use of candlewick was restricted to bedspreads, but it looks effective in many other forms and can be used for cushions, rugs and bath mats as well as for warm garments such as dressing gowns.

The trace design given in this chapter is adaptable for almost any use and builds up extremely well, placing the motifs as linking squares. It can be used for both tufted and smooth types of candlewicking and parts of the design might be adapted for a matching border motif.

Materials for candlewick

There are two kinds of candlewicking, tufted and smooth, but for both types it is essential that the material on which the embroidery is worked should shrink on the first washing to secure the candlewick in the fabric.

Usually, bleached calico is used for candlewick, but linen can also be used. It is important to choose a weave which will take two thicknesses of the candlewick cotton.

Yarn. Twilleys Lyscot cotton is used for candlewick and is sold in skeins, available in a variety of colours. Skeins can be cut into 48 inch lengths or, if preferred, wind the yarn into a ball and use as required.

Needles. A special candlewick needle is used; this is large sized with a flattened, curved point and a big eye.

Scissors. It is essential to have scissors which are extremely sharp for cutting the loops. A blunt pair will drag and pull the tufts out of the fabric.

Designs

Designs for candlewick are most effective when based on geometric shapes, but flowing designs can also be used if they are large sized. Small, intricate patterns are difficult to work and the shapes become distorted with the tufting. The candlewick can follow the outlines of the design, can fill in some areas, or cover the background completely as an all over design, giving a solid area of pile texture.

Tufted candlewick

In some early examples of candlewick French knots and backstitch were used, but in modern embroidery the stitch mainly used is running stitch worked $\frac{1}{4}$ inch—$\frac{1}{2}$ inch apart along the line of the

170

▲ *A trace design for working in either tufted or smooth candlewicking*

▲ *A detail of the design above worked in tufted stitch and showing the reverse*

design, leaving a small loop between each stitch. To keep the loops of even length place a pencil under the cotton as each loop is made. The candlewick yarn is used double. Cut a length twice as long as is required and thread it through the needle until the ends are level. It is not necessary to finish off the ends when starting or finishing—begin on the right side of the fabric, leaving an end equal to the size of the completed tuft and end in the same way.

When all the design is completely worked cut the loops evenly with a very sharp pair of scissors.

Smooth candlewick

This type of candlewick is worked simply in running stitch. One doubled length of cotton is used in the needle as for tufted candlewick and the stitches are worked about $\frac{1}{4}$ inch long and $\frac{1}{4}$ inch apart. This results in a bead-like stitch giving a beautifully raised, sculptured effect. This type of candlewick is at its best worked in geometric designs built up into solid shapes and covering the entire area of the fabric.

Finishing candlewick

The completed work should be washed so

▲ Smooth candlewicking in a modern bedspread

that the fabric shrinks to fix the tufts more securely and to fluff them up. If a washing machine is used, wash for at least 20 minutes in warm soapy water. If washing by hand let the work soak for three to four hours. Do not wring or squeeze, just shake out.

Dry the work out of doors in a strong breeze and shake it frequently whilst drying to eliminate creasing and to make the tufts fluffier. Brush the tufts lightly with a soft brush before they are quite dry to fluff them up.

It is best to avoid ironing candlewick as this will flatten the tufts.

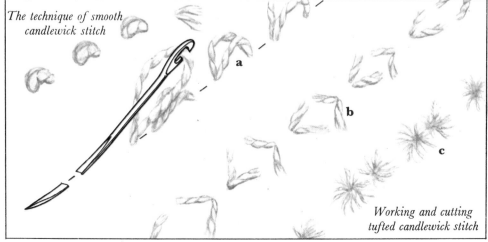

The technique of smooth candlewick stitch

Working and cutting tufted candlewick stitch

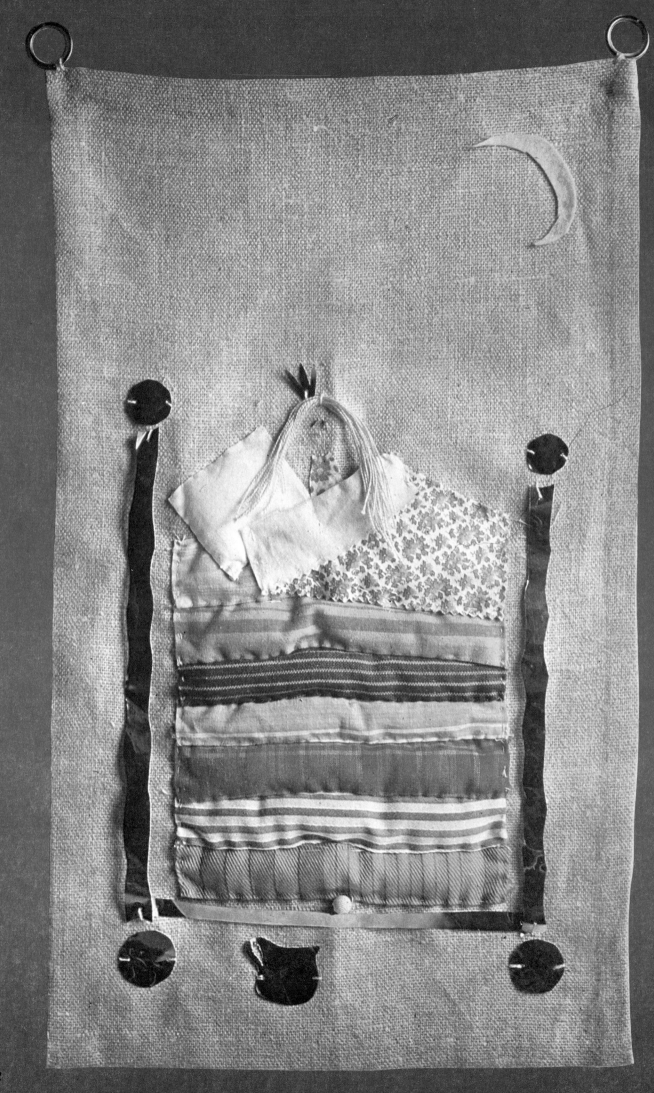

Stitchery pattern/fairy tale in embroidery

This delightful embroidery hanging illustrates the old fairy tale 'The princess and the pea'—and there she is, uncomfortably feeling the pea through seven mattresses. It's simple to do and a young embroiderer might be encouraged to work it for her own bedroom wall.

The mattress pieces are stitched to the background on three sides, leaving the top open. Insert a small amount of teased-out cotton wool to pad the mattress and close the top with running stitches. Metal foil has been used for the bed frame, the chamber pot and the princess's crown. Cut out the shapes and then prick the stitching holes with a needle.

The foil shapes must be stitched very loosely to the background or the foil will be damaged by the stitches. The pea is a small white bead, stitched finally under the bottom mattress.

After hemming all four sides of the hanging, stitch two curtain rings to the upper corners.

The hanging illustrated was worked to a measurement of 13 inches deep by 8½ inches wide.

▼ Two more fairy stories which would make companion wall panels, Thumbelina and the Little Mermaid

Costume design/19th century ladies

The main features of this costume from the 1800's are the high Empire waistline and the tubular dress skirt with its elaborate hem decoration. This was a graceful and feminine look and very flattering.

The Dress
The dress has a high waistline with a narrow waistband joining the skirt to the bodice. The skirt is gathered very slightly at the front and more fully at the back, standing away at the hem and finishing above the ankles.

Neck lines of this period were either high and worn with puffed sleeves ending well below the wrist, or low with the puffed sleeves ending above the elbow. A frilled muslin neckerchief was worn to fill the low neckline. A Spencer was usually worn over the thin dress for warmth.

Fabrics and colours
Muslin, fine linen and cotton, embroidered or printed with spots, sprigs of flowers, and delicate border prints on white were most popular for day dresses, although soft pastel shades came in later in the period. For evening wear, gauze over coloured silk or satin was fashionable. Outer garments were made from woollen or silk cloth; the Spencer was usually either blue or black.

Accessories
Bags of silk (bead embroidered or tubular knitted silk) were carried by ladies, and parasols, short gloves and small fans were necessary to complete an evening outfit.

Shoes were very pointed with tiny curved heels or no heels at all, worn with flesh or white coloured stockings.

Hats and hair
Hats were richly trimmed; turbans, berets and tall crowned bonnets were adorned with frills, rosettes, ostrich feathers and ribbons etc. Mob caps which covered the hair and framed the face were worn indoors. Hair was centrally parted and arranged in curls on the temples with short ringlets and curls at the front and sides.

19th Century costume

You will need
The dress. 4 yards 36 inch wide material; cotton lawn, voile, muslin or any soft light fabric, white, pastel or sprigged on white. Ribbons, flowers etc for decorating the hem.

The Spencer. 2 yards 36 inch wide coatweight woollen cloth, blue or black.

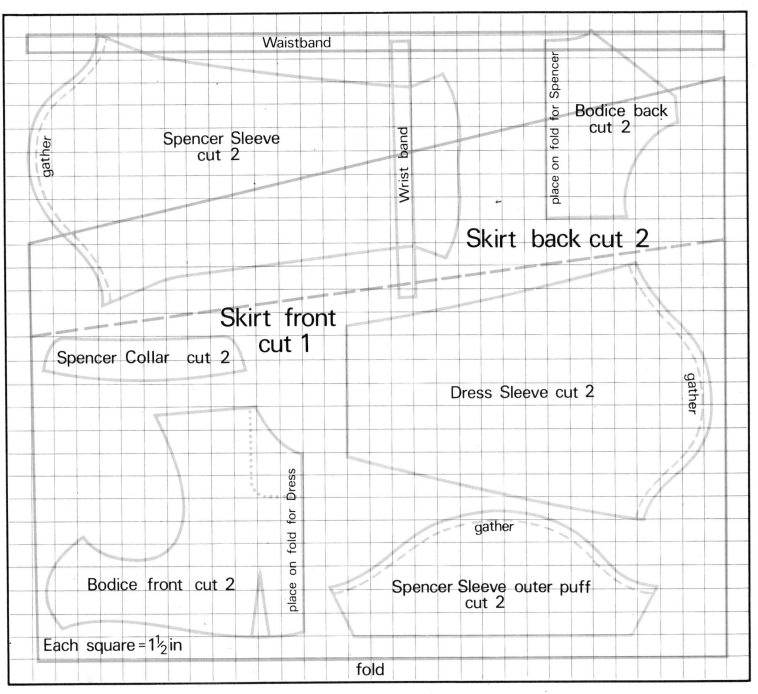

Each square = 1½ in

Waistband

Spencer Sleeve
cut 2

gather

Wrist band

place on fold for Spencer

Bodice back
cut 2

Skirt back cut 2

Skirt front
cut 1

Spencer Collar   cut 2

Dress Sleeve cut 2

gather

place on fold for Dress

Bodice front cut 2

gather

Spencer Sleeve outer puff
cut 2

fold

Matching braid.
(The graph pattern will fit 34 inch bust.)

To make the dress
Make a paper pattern from the graph and separate the pieces of pattern.
Place the Skirt Front on the fabric folded lengthwise and cut out. Cut two Skirt Backs, without cutting on the fold, and join front to backs. Seam the centre back leaving an opening 8 inches long at the waist.
Place Bodice Front on fold and cut out. Cut two Bodice Backs. Make the waist-bust darts on the bodice front. Join side seams and shoulder seams.
Leave centre back open. Cut the Waistband on the straight of the fabric, to diaphram measurement plus turnings. Sew to the bodice leaving the waist back open. Gather the waist edge of the skirt, gently at the front and more fully at the back. Join the skirt to the waistband, still

leaving the back of the bodice and skirt waist open.
Gather the top of the Sleeve pieces with running stitches. Sew the underarm seam, and pin the sleeves into position, the gathers at the top of the sleeve. Sew the sleeves in.
Face the neck, hem and cuffs. Sew concealed hooks and eyes down the back opening. Adjust the hem length and sew.

To make the Spencer
Cut out one Bodice Back, placing it on along the fold of the fabric as indicated on the chart. Cut out two Bodice Fronts. Join the pieces on side and shoulder seams, leaving the front open. Face the front edges with self fabric.
Cut a strip 3 inches wide and long enough to fit the diaphragm measurement on the cross. Fold this to 1½ inches wide and bind the waist edge of the Spencer.
Cut two collar sections in fabric and two

in interfacing. Make up the collar and attach to the neck line adjusting to fit comfortably. Sew hooks and eyes to close the Spencer front edge to edge.
To make up the Spencer sleeves, cut out the outer puff section twice and the whole sleeve twice. Gather the top edge of the outer puff section with two rows of stitches and adjust to fit the armhole. Fasten off the thread. Sew the underarm seam. Sew a narrow hem along the puff edge cuff.
Stitch a strip of braid across the sleeve wrists of the main Spencer sleeves where indicated on the chart. Gather the top of the sleeve and adjust to fit the armhole. Sew the underarm seams. Finish off the cuff edge. Slip the puff over the main sleeve, pin both into the armhole and sew.
To complete the look of the period, a roll is made by gathering a 10 inch long by 3 inch deep length of taffeta and stitching it to the inside back waist to lift the skirt.

Tailoring three

In this chapter
A. Canvassing the front and back:
padding the front canvas; basting canvas
to the front; basting canvas to the back;
adding a bridle; front stay tape; finishing
the canvassing.
B. Piped buttonholes: marking the
buttonholes; making the buttonholes.
C. Pockets with lining: interfacing a
pocket; straight piped pocket; shaped
piped pocket; piped flap pocket; flap
pocket; false flap pocket; welt pocket.
D. Lining a pocket
* Terms and stitches

A. Canvassing the front and back

The canvas is sewn in place after any
style seams, darts and back seams have
been stitched but before the shoulder
seams and side seams are stitched.

Padding the front canvas
After stitching the darts or seams on
the canvas (see Tailoring 1, D) trim off
the seam allowance plus $\frac{1}{16}$ inch on
the underarm, armhole and shoulder to
reduce bulk in seams.
1a, b, c. For a perfect result add a chest
pad of felt or domette, stitched to the
canvas by staggered rows of pad stitching*.
This does not add bulk but gives a rounded
line to the chest.
The padding is stitched to the side of the
canvas which faces the lining.

Basting canvas to the front
Lay the canvas flat on a table, padded
side down. Over it lay the corresponding
coat front with the wrong side of the coat
fabric facing the canvas.
Match and pin the centre and crease lines
together.
2a, b. Baste the following:
(i) Working from the bust line upwards
baste the front edges of the coat to the
canvas, smoothing it up while working to
prevent wrinkles.
(ii) Repeat from the bust line downwards.
(iii) Baste the opposite edge of the canvas
in a line from the hem through the bust up
to shoulder.
(iv) Baste round the armhole and along
the shoulder.
(v) Finally, baste along the crease line
of the lapel.

*A wrap-around coat and jacket in luxury
fabrics. The jacket, Butterick pattern number
6528, is made up in cashmere and features
raglan sleeves and a topstitched step collar.
The coat, Butterick pattern number 6518, is
made up in 100% angora with a Prince of
Wales check*

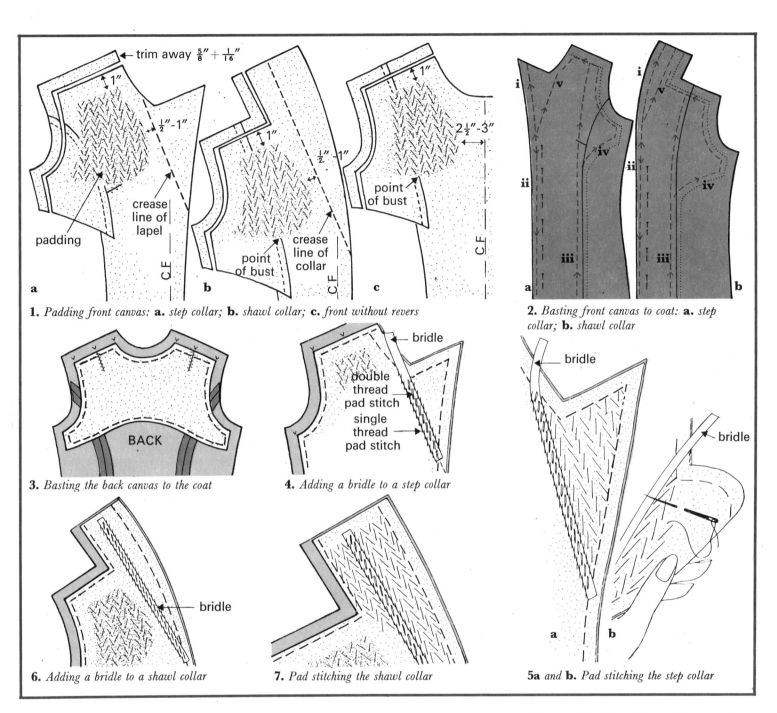

1. *Padding front canvas:* **a.** *step collar;* **b.** *shawl collar;* **c.** *front without revers*

2. *Basting front canvas to coat:* **a.** *step collar;* **b.** *shawl collar*

3. *Basting the back canvas to the coat*

4. *Adding a bridle to a step collar*

6. *Adding a bridle to a shawl collar*

7. *Pad stitching the shawl collar*

5a and **b.** *Pad stitching the step collar*

Basting canvas to the back

Trim off the seam allowance plus $\frac{1}{16}$ inch round underarm, armhole, shoulder and neck edges.

Stitch any darts or seams. Even if you have decided to dispense with the back shoulder dart and ease in the shoulder seam instead, you should make the dart on the canvas.

3. Baste canvas to the wrong side of the coat back as shown, easing the coat fabric to the canvas along the back shoulder seam if necessary.

Adding a bridle

A bridle is a piece of $\frac{1}{2}$ inch wide linen tape sewn to the canvas along the roll line of a lapel, continuing into the step collar for 2 inches or to the centre back for a shawl collar.

The linen tape should be shrunk by damp pressing or washing before application to prevent more shrinkage later.

Step collar. Cut a piece of tape to the length of the crease line plus 2 inches to extend into the collar.

4. Pin tape centrally along the crease line with 2 inches extending at the neck edge. Keep the tape taut.

Using a double, matching silk thread, pad stitch the tape in place along the centre. This gives a strong central line. Then, with single silk thread, pad stitch along each edge.

5a, b. Starting from the bridle work rows of staggered pad stitching towards the edge. Keep the rows in line with the

bridle and don't sew beyond the seam line. Hold the lapel in a curled position with the left hand.

Shawl collar. Cut a piece of tape to the length of the crease line.

6. Pin tape centrally along the crease line keeping it taut. Using a double matching silk thread, pad stitch the tape in place along the centre. Then, with single thread, pad stitch along each edge.

7. Starting from the bridle, work rows of pad stitching towards the edge. Shape the rows slightly at outer edge to allow the collar to set correctly, and don't sew beyond the seam line.

While working, roll the collar in a curled position with the left hand as for the step collar (**5b**).

Front stay tape

8a, b, c. Stay tape is sewn to the front edges. On a coat with a step collar the tape extends from the hem to the top of the crease line (**a**) and on a coat with a shawl collar from hem to centre back (**b**). On any other style the tape is taken up the front to the neck edge (**c**).

9. Before adding the stay tape work as follows:

Trim the front edge of the canvas just within the sewing line to reduce bulk.

Cut linen tape to the required length.

Position the tape and baste the strip taut at the outer edge.

Catch stitch* the inner edge to the canvas.

Finishing the canvassing

Finally, catch stitch the canvas to the coat at the underarm, shoulder and arm-hole on both back and front. Take care not to pull the stitches tight.

Working on the wrong side press well up to the crease line. Fold back along the crease line and allow the collar to roll, but do not press.

B. Piped buttonholes

There are several ways of making fabric buttonholes. For the heavier weight fabrics used in tailoring the following method is very successful.

Marking the buttonholes

The buttonhole length is the diameter of the button plus $\frac{1}{8}$ inch. If you buy the size of button suggested in the pattern then the buttonhole markings will be correct, otherwise re-mark, moving the inside tailor's tacks.

10. To ensure that the buttonholes are in line and parallel to each other, prepare tram-lines on the markings, tacking through both fabric and canvas. Remove the tailor's tacks.

Making the buttonholes

For each buttonhole cut two pipes in the coat fabric. The pipes should be 1 inch wide and the length of the buttonhole plus $1\frac{1}{2}$ inches, cut in the straight grain of the fabric.

11. Position the pipes on the right side of the garment, with the edges meeting along the buttonhole line and right sides facing. Baste.

Chalk mark the ends of the buttonhole.

12. Working on the right side, stitch along the buttonhole length to each side of the buttonhole marking. The lines should be $\frac{1}{4}$ inch apart for buttonholes (and $\frac{1}{2}$ inch apart for pockets). At each end of the stitching over stitch for about $\frac{1}{2}$ inch to secure ends.

178

Remove the tram-lines.

13. Working on the wrong side, cut along the buttonhole line making deep mitred v's at the corners at least $\frac{3}{8}$ inch deep. Take care not to cut the pipes.

14. Pull the pipes through the opening to the wrong side. Press the seams open, and the mitres away from the buttonhole.

15. Working on the right side adjust the pipes into even folds and oversew to close. Stab stitch* along the seam line as shown.

16. At the back work an oversewing stitch at each end of the buttonhole to hold the facing in position.

17. Fold garment back and back stitch through pipes and mitre as near to the fold as possible.

C. Pockets with lining

Pockets can be functional or decorative. The right place for them varies for each figure so make sure at the first fitting that they are in the right position for you.

Interfacing a pocket

All pocket openings are interfaced with a strip of silesia, or duck, basted on the wrong side of the opening to support them.

18. Cut the interfacing with the grain falling along the line of the pocket where possible, and take it into a seam where practicable. Position and baste to the wrong side of the pocket opening, then make up the pocket as follows.

19. Straight piped pocket

This type of pocket looks well if made with contrast pipes. The average pocket length for a coat is $5\frac{1}{2}$ inches to 6 inches. For each pocket cut two pipes 2 inches wide and to the pocket length plus $1\frac{1}{2}$ inches, in the straight grain of the fabric. Make the pocket opening as for bound buttonholes (B), but with the stitching lines $\frac{1}{2}$ inch apart.

To finish, add the pocket backing and lining as shown in D.

20. Shaped piped pocket

Mark pocket position carefully with basting. Then interface the back.

21. To pipe the pocket cut a piece of fabric suitable for the pocket shape as shown, using coat or contrast fabric. Position the piece of material, right sides facing, over the marked pocket opening, matching any design or check if appropriate.

Baste in place along pocket line.

22. Stitch carefully at equal distances from the basting. The width depends on how you would like the pocket to look.

23. Cut through patch only, as shown, to make pipes.

24. Cut through garment along pocket

8. *Stay tape stitched to front of coat with: a. step collar; b. shawl collar; c. coat without revers*

opening, mitring corners.

Finish as for a straight piped pocket, snipping any curved seams.

Finally, add the pocket lining and backing as shown in D.

25. Piped flap pocket

Make a piped pocket without lining.

26. From the coat fabric cut a pocket flap to the length of the finished pocket and to the desired shape of flap, plus 1 inch on all edges for seam allowance. Cut a lining for the flap to match.

27. Place pieces together, right sides facing, and stitch as shown. Snip across the corners.

28. Turn to the right side and press, then draw a chalk line 1 inch from the raw edge as shown.

29. Slip flap under top pipe and baste in place through all layers along the stitching line of the top pipe.

30. Turn to the wrong side and stitch in place over the original seam at the back of the top pipe.

To finish, add the pocket backing and lining as shown in D.

31. Flap pocket

Make up the flap as for a piped flap pocket (figures 26, 27 and 28) and cut one pipe as for a straight piped pocket.

Interface the wrong side of the pocket opening.

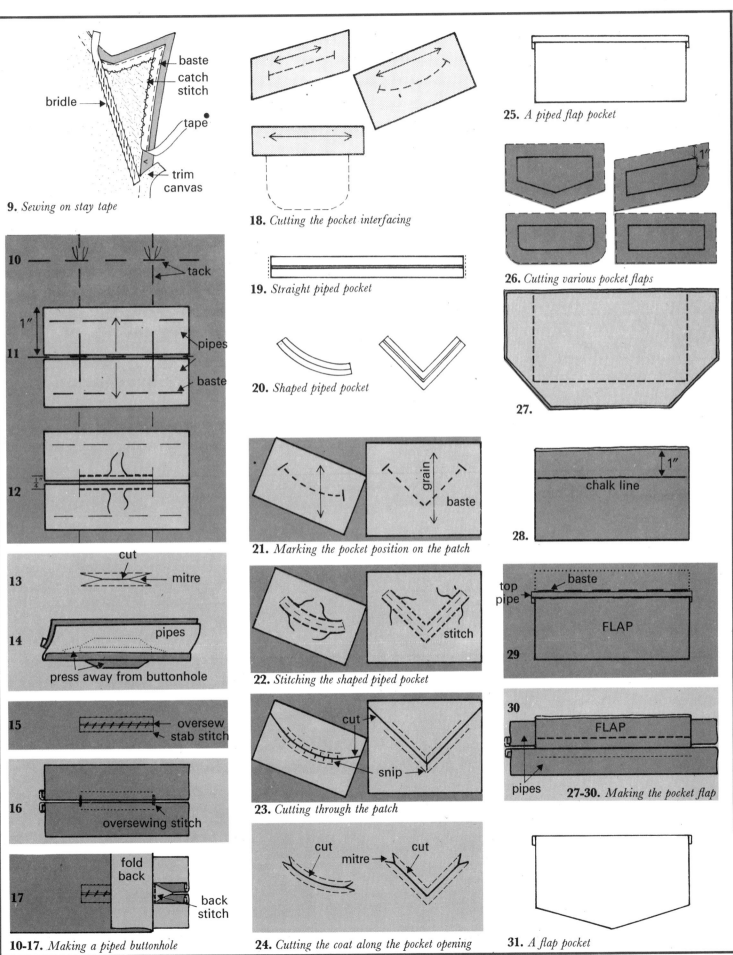

9. *Sewing on stay tape*

baste
catch stitch
bridle
tape
trim canvas

10
tack

11
1″
pipes
baste

12
¼″

13
cut
mitre

14
pipes
press away from buttonhole

15
oversew
stab stitch

16
oversewing stitch

17
fold back
back stitch

10-17. *Making a piped buttonhole*

18. *Cutting the pocket interfacing*

19. *Straight piped pocket*

20. *Shaped piped pocket*

21. *Marking the pocket position on the patch*
grain
baste

22. *Stitching the shaped piped pocket*
stitch

23. *Cutting through the patch*
cut
snip

24. *Cutting the coat along the pocket opening*
cut
mitre
cut

25. *A piped flap pocket*

26. *Cutting various pocket flaps*
1″

27.

28.
1″
chalk line

29
top pipe
baste
FLAP

30
FLAP
pipes

27-30. *Making the pocket flap*

31. *A flap pocket*

179

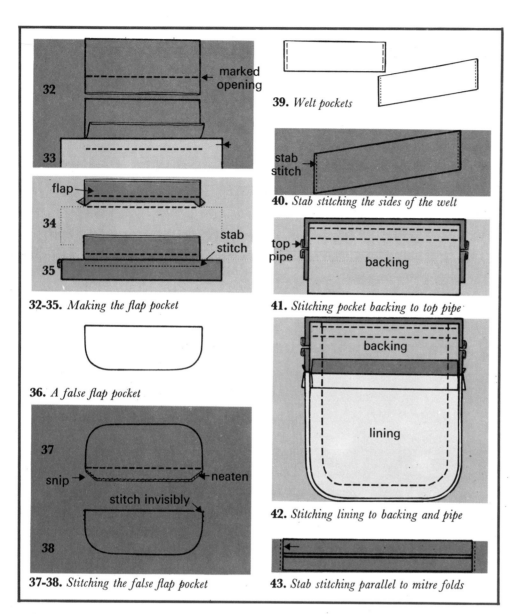

32-35. *Making the flap pocket*

36. *A false flap pocket*

37-38. *Stitching the false flap pocket*

39. *Welt pockets*

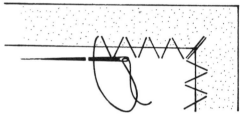

40. *Stab stitching the sides of the welt*

41. *Stitching pocket backing to top pipe*

42. *Stitching lining to backing and pipe*

43. *Stab stitching parallel to mitre folds*

32. Stitch the flap in place along the marked pocket opening, with right side facing.

33. Fold the flap seam up, out of the way, and stitch the bottom pipe in place as for a piped buttonhole.
Cut through the back of the opening as for a piped buttonhole.

34. Turn the flap seam allowance through the opening to the wrong side, leaving the flap on the right side. Press the flap seam allowance up and the mitres away from the opening.

35. Pipe the lower seam opening as for a piped buttonhole.
To finish, add the pocket backing and lining as shown in step D.

36. False flap pocket
Make a flap as for a piped flap pocket. (figures 26, 27 and 28).

37. Position over opening and stitch. Cut away corners and neaten raw edge.

38. Press the flap down and fasten the sides carefully.

39. Welt pocket
Make up the welt as for the flap in figures 26, 27 and 28. Then make up as for a flap pocket but placing the welt to the lower edge and piping the top edge.

40. Finish the backing and lining as in D. Press the welt up and stab stitch* in place. If the coat is finished with top stitching you can topstitch the sides instead of stab stitching them.

D. Lining a pocket

41. Cut a backing for the pocket in coat fabric, 3 inches deep and to the length of the pipe. Stitch to the top pipe or flap seam allowance as near as possible to the original stitching line. For added strength stitch again ½ inch above first row.

42. For each pocket cut two pieces of lining fabric 4 inches deep and to the length of the pipe. Stitch one piece of lining to the lower edge of the backing and the other piece to the bottom pipe or welt seam allowance.
Round off the lower edges of the lining as shown then stitch round to make the pocket.

43. Working on the right side stab stitch parallel to the mitre folds for added strength.

---

*Terms and stitches

Catch stitch (44). Used to catch one fabric to another where bulk is to be avoided. Lift one thread of fabric with each stitch so as to be invisible on right side. Do not pull stitches tight.

Pad stitching (45). Worked as shown, the needle to be at right angles to the stitching line. Work with an imaginary grid, coming down one line and going up the next, without turning the work. Stagger the stitches to prevent pleats being formed.
Use small stitches (about ¼-½ inch long) for stitching canvas to lapel and collar to create a roll.
Use medium stitches (about 1 inch long) for lashing padding to canvas.
Use large stitches (about 2 inches long) for quick basting.

Stab stitch (46). Used where almost invisible stitches are needed to hold fabric layers together firmly.
a. Working from the right side, push needle down vertically, pull needle through from wrong side.
b. Then push needle up vertically and pull through from right side.
The stitches should be very small.

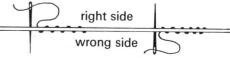

right side

wrong side

Crafts/weaving

An introduction to weaving

Weaving is one of the oldest handcrafts known to man, yet the basic techniques have changed hardly at all since earliest times. It's a craft that almost anyone can master without difficulty, whatever their age—the rag weaving examples shown on this page were worked by children.

Weaving is basically a very simple craft requiring a frame to hold the threads taut so that other threads can be interlaced at right angles.

There are several different kinds of looms and weaving frames available in craft shops. Each of them is designed in a different way to enable the weaver to interlace the yarns in the easiest manner according to the type of fabric to be woven.

The simplest weaving structure of all is a frame card, a piece of card notched at opposite ends with the warp threads strung between them. This will produce small pieces of woven fabric. At the other end of the scale, a beginner can learn to weave on a four-shaft loom with equal

▲ *Study this picture of the finished frame loom before starting to make it. You will get a clearer idea of the use of various parts*

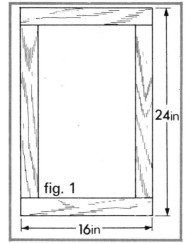

fig. 1

24in

16in

fig. 2

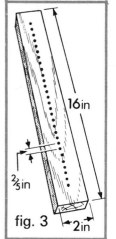

16in

²⁄₃in

fig. 3

2in

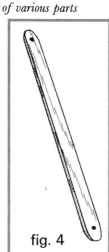

fig. 4

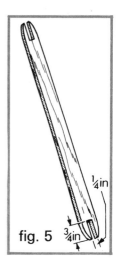

¼in

³⁄₄in

fig. 5

chances of success, and produce all kinds of woven fabrics for wall hangings, rugs, mats, table runners, clothes and accessories. As an introduction to this fascinating and absorbing craft, this chapter gives instructions for making a simple frame loom and setting it up for weaving, and suggests some ideas for using the woven fabric.

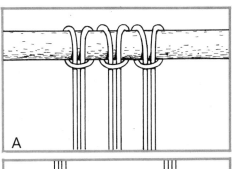

Glossary of weaving terms

Warp. Threads stretched lengthwise on a loom.
Weft. The cross threads woven into the warp.
Shed. The wedge-shaped opening, created when alternate warp threads are raised or lowered; the space where the weft yarn travels across the warp.
Raddle. (Sometimes called the 'reed'). A comb-like implement for separating the warp threads and 'beating up' the weft.
Leashes. Strings tied to groups of warp threads, to pull them up to make a shed.
Draft. The way in which the loom is threaded up.
Shed Stick. An implement which, when turned on its side, makes a shed for the weft threads to pass through.
Weaving Stick. The implement upon which the weft yarn is wound and which is used to pass the weft threads through the sheds.

A simple frame loom

To make the loom you will need:
- [ ] Planed timber 10ft x 2in x 1in
- [ ] Planed timber 4ft 6in x 1in x ¼in
- [ ] 3ft of ½in dowelling rod
- [ ] 4 brass 1¼in hooks
- [ ] 8 1¼in No. 6 screws
- [ ] ½lb 2½in round head nails

Constructing the frame
Cut the timber into required sizes:
- [ ] 3 lengths 16 inches long and 2 lengths 24 inches long from the 2in x 1in timber.
- [ ] 3 lengths 18 inches long from the 1in x ¼in timber.

Stage 1. Place two 16 inch lengths across two 24 inch lengths to make a frame. Make sure the corners are absolutely square and screw the four pieces together,

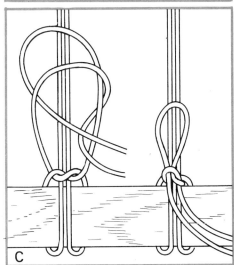

using two screws on each corner (figure 1).
Stage 2. Bore a hole in each corner of the frame between the screw heads, using a bradawl. Screw in the hooks so that the open end of the hook faces outwards (figure 2).
Stage 3. Cut the length of dowelling rod in half. This is used to make the rods on which the warp threads are tied. The hooks hold the rods in position (see illustration of completed frame loom).
The Raddle. Draw a line down the centre of the remaining 16 inch length of wood. Leaving approximately 1 inch at either end, mark points along the centre line at ⅖ inch intervals. Drill ⅛ inch holes approximately ¼ inch deep at each point. Insert a nail in each hole and tap them home until they are firmly embedded. Do not hammer or the wood may split (figure 3).
Shed stick. Take two of the 18 inch lengths of wood and drill an ⅛ inch hole at both ends of each piece, one inch in from the end. Round off and smooth the ends of both pieces (figure 4).
Weaving stick or wooden shuttle. Using the remaining 18 inch length of wood, cut slots into each end 1 inch deep by ¼ inch wide as shown in figure 5.

Setting up the loom

Putting on the warp
Cut warp threads twice the length of the weaving frame (48 inches) plus 10 inches and tie them onto one of the warp rods in the way shown in diagram A, making sure that the ends are of equal length. Space them evenly along the rod.
With a narrow end of the frame towards you, hook the rod into place at the far end of the frame and then tie the warp ends onto the front rod as follows: working from the centre take a pair of warp threads and pull them taut over and under the front rod and tie in a single knot as shown in diagram B. This first knot will hold the warp rod in place at the front of the frame while you continue knotting all the warp threads. Make sure that the tension is even. When all the pairs of warp threads are tied, complete the knot as shown in diagram C.
The warp threads are now complete.
Making the first shed. Put the shed stick in position at the top of the frame by sliding it over the first right hand warp thread and under the first left warp thread and working thus across the loom (diagram D). Tie the shed stick with a piece of string through the end holes to prevent it falling out of the loom. When this stick is turned on its side it makes a shed for the weft threads to pass through.

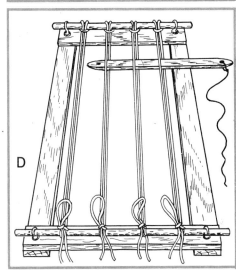

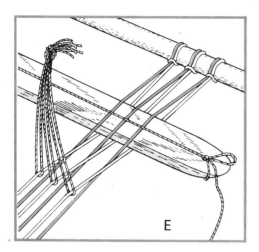

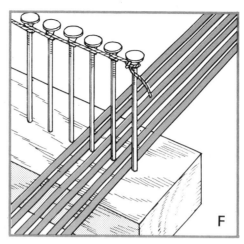

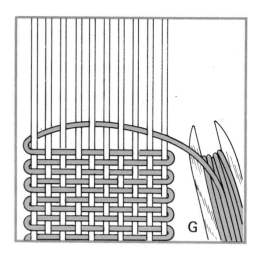

Making the second shed. The second shed is made using leashes and for these use a ball of soft firm string—rough string would damage the warp threads. Cut the required number of strings 18 inches long. Loop a piece of string under one of the right hand warp threads just in front of the shed stick. Knot the ends of the leash together evenly. Knot two more right hand warp threads and then knot the leashes together in groups of three about 4 inches above the warp threads (see diagram E). Tie the remaining leashes across the loom in the same way. The second shed is made by holding the grouped leashes firmly and lifting them so that the weft threads can pass through the space.

Plain weave

To produce a plain weave first one series of warp threads is lifted by turning the shed stick onto its side and then alternate threads are lifted on the groups of leashes. This means that (by counting from the right) the shed stick lifts even numbered warp threads and the leashes lift odd numbered warp threads.

The raddle

The raddle spaces the warp threads evenly and is also used to beat the weft threads into position. Place the raddle on the loom in front of the leashes so that the warp threads go through the spaces between the nails in pairs. Then loop a piece of soft string round each nail to keep the warp ends from jumping out of position (see diagram F). The frame loom is now ready for the weaving to commence.

Yarns

Because the frame loom has a fairly coarse construction, it is better to use a fairly thick yarn for the warp. Thick rug wool or thick soft string would be suitable for the first attempt at weaving. Finer

yarns or mixed textures can be used when a little experience has been gained. It is important when choosing the warp yarn not to use anything that breaks or fluffs too easily.

Suitable weft yarns are cotton, wool, linen and string. For fun and more exciting effects try weaving with strips of paper, grass, rushes, cane, dried plants, lengths of beads, lace, ribbon, pieces of thin wood, or strips of coloured fabric. Remember when using different yarns and colours to exaggerate the contrast to achieve the most interesting results.

Starting to weave

Wind the weft yarn onto the weaving stick, making sure that it does not get too fat because it is then awkward to use. Turn the shed stick onto its side so that it makes a shed and slide the second shed stick through the space in front of the raddle. Holding the raddle parallel with the front of the frame, pull it firmly towards you until it can go no further. By putting the stick in at the beginning of the weaving you make sure that the warp ends lie evenly spaced for making an even textured cloth (see diagram G). You are now ready to begin using the weft yarn, which is passed through so that it lies in an arc on the warp threads and is then beaten evenly into position again at the front shed stick with the raddle. Lift the leashes and pass the weft through the shed. Begin and end weft threads in exactly the same way, by hooking the thread around the outside warp thread.

It is essential to keep the weaving the same width all the time and this is done by making sure that the weft threads are not pulled too tight. This is why the weft threads are left in an arc before being beaten into place and not pulled in a straight line across the cloth.

When the weaving is complete remove the leashes, the shed sticks and the raddle,

untie the half knots at one end and slide the rod from the other end.

Finishing warp thread ends

For mats the ends of the cloth can either be hemmed and fringed or knotted and fringed.

Weaves

On this draft plain weaves are woven but by free weaving (ie lifting the warp threads individually by hand and not using the shed stick and leashes) a greater variety of woven effects can be achieved. Free weaving is used when substances other than yarns are used for the weft.

Things to make

Shoulder bag

Weave brightly coloured stripes of plain weave. Remove the work from the loom and sew up the sides. Fringe the warp ends to make an interesting border at the top of the bag. Add a cord for the handle and line the bag with a firm material. For a different effect, weave an inlay pattern on a plain background. Knot the warp ends together to form a side seam and sew up one side for the base of the bag. Add a handle and line with fabric.

Mats

Make a set of mats in plain weave stripes, varying the combination of colours or textures for each mat. Fringe the edges. Rushes, canes, raffia, or string can be used for interesting textures but remember that the mats must be cleanable.

Wall hangings

One can experiment and use different kinds of yarns and all kinds of objects to make wall hangings because they don't have to withstand wear and tear. If a great deal of colour is required, keep the texture and weave simple. If rich texture is the aim, use very simple colours.

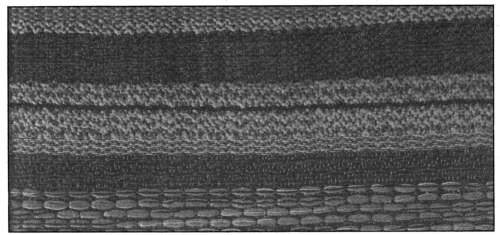

▲ *Fine jute warp, weft of mixed wool and worsted*   ▼ *Plain weave, 4 thin warp threads woven as one*

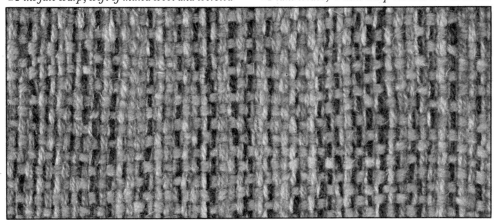

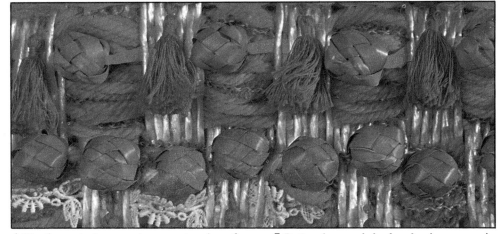

▲ *Plastic warp; lace, wool, rayon, tassels weft*   ▼ *Pattern here made by free darning on weaving*

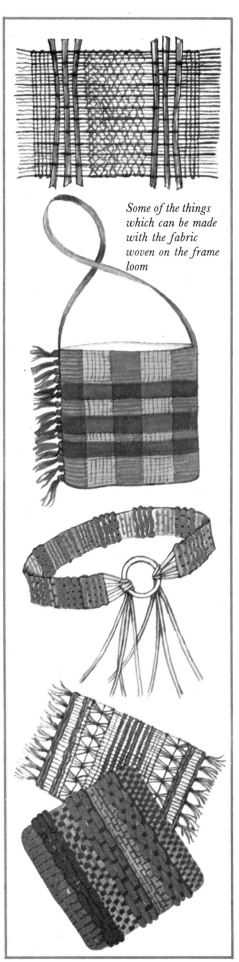

Some of the things which can be made with the fabric woven on the frame loom

Machine knitting/home furnishings

Although fabrics suitable for home furnishings can be knitted on non-automatic machines, the semi-automatic and fully-automatic models, which have a much wider range of two-colour patterns and have knit-weave facilities, can produce a very varied range of textures, from fine lace for curtains to crunchy weaves suitable for rugs.

The room settings illustrated in this chapter use fabrics knitted on a Knitmaster 321 punch card machine, but the ideas could easily be adapted to other types of knitting machines.

Curtains are simple to make and can be made from fine yarns worked in lace patterns or in thicker yarns to produce tapestry or brocade-like effects. In the blue and green bedroom illustrated in the last chapter the same pattern was used for both the curtains and the bedspread. The lacey effect was achieved by working a Fair Isle type pattern but instead of a second colour an invisible thread was used.

Some knitting machines have an attachment which makes lace fabric using only one yarn. The Jones model 558, for instance, has a second carriage which automatically transfers a stitch from one needle to its neighbouring needle, thus achieving a 'knit together and make one' action which, in various combinations, makes pretty lace fabrics.

The bedspread in the blue and green setting was made quite simply from a single wide length, with another length of fabric gathered onto the edge for the skirt.

Using motifs for a theme

Both the curtains and the bedspread in the child's room setting are made from straight lengths of fabric, and use a linking bold motif of a giraffe. The bedspread and bedhead is worked as one piece with the motif worked at the foot end of the spread and again at the other end for a bedhead. Two rings have been attached, one on each corner, to hook the bedhead to the wall.

Varying textures

The fabrics in the sitting room setting are worked in shades of brown and cream, varying in texture from the smooth two-colour fabric of the cushion covers to the thick weave of the wall panel. The patterned material was worked in one length and then cut and stitched to make tailored fitting covers. Piping is easily made on a knitting machine and could be used for edging the cushions.

At the top of the wall hanging a deep

◄ *Nursery with bedspread and curtains fabric knitted on Knitmaster model 321*

▲ *Room setting for a sitting room; wall hanging, rug and the fabric for the seat are knitted on a Knitmaster punch card model 321*

band of stocking stitch was worked, turned to the wrong side and then sewn in place to form a casing for the supporting rod. An alternative method of hanging the panel might be to attach ornamental rings along the top edge. The lower edge of the panel can be decorated with a plaited, woven or macramé fringe.

The rug which uses the knit-weaving technique is backed with hessian to strengthen it, but any suitable iron-on backing would do, remembering that a wool rug is inclined to slip underfoot on a polished floor. The trim used on the wall panel could be used to edge the rug, or a purchased fringed trim could be stitched to both edges or all round.

Other uses for straight pieces

Cushions of all shapes and sizes are suitable projects for machine knitted home accessories, and lend themselves to interesting use of pattern and colour. Stool covers, fire screens and lampshades can also be made from knitted fabrics, as well as rugs of different kinds. To make an attractive rya-type bedroom rug, for example, cast on ten stitches in the centre of the needle bed and then cast on five stitches six inches away from centre to the right and another five six inches to the left. Knitting on this arrangement of needles produces a long strip of fabric which, when the sides are folded to the centre, makes a strip of loops. Stitch

strips along the centre in rows onto a piece of straight knitting to make a rug. Lengths of knitted fabric can also be used in garment making and is a practical way of making matching jumper and skirt ensembles. Supposing a knitter has decided upon a leaf green jumper and would like a skirt in a leaf green and blue mixture fabric to match. She simply knits her jumper and then knits up a length of two-colour fabric, and uses it in the same way as she would a length of woven material, pinning a paper pattern to it and cutting out the garment pieces. When choosing a paper pattern for machine knitted fabric select one designed for use with jersey material.

187

Crochet pattern/belted trouser suit

This unusually styled crochet suit will be an extremely useful addition to any wardrobe. The jacket has a heavily textured stitch which is repeated in a band round the foot of the trousers. The remainder of the trousers is worked in treble. A belt has been added for extra style.

Sizes
To fit 32[35]in bust
Jacket. Length, 27[27½]in
Sleeve seam, 15in
Trousers. Inside leg, 30in adjustable

Tension for this design
10tr to 3in worked on No.4·50 hook
15 bean sts to 8in and 3 bean st rows to 2in

Materials shown here
Sirdar Studio
24[28] balls
One No.4·50 (ISR) crochet hook
8 buttons
⅜yd elastic

Trousers left leg

Begin at waistline and using No.4·50 hook, make 52[56]ch.
1st row 1tr into 4th ch from hook, 1tr into each ch to end. 50[54] sts.
2nd row 3ch to count as first tr, 1tr into each tr to end. Continue in tr, inc one st at each end of 5th and every following 5th row until there are 56[60] sts.
Continue without shaping until work measures 10in.

Shape crutch
Next row 8ch, turn, 1tr into 4th ch from hook, 1tr into each of next 4ch, 1tr into each st to end, join a separate length of yarn to the end of the row, work 5ch and break off, then with original yarn work 1tr into each of 5ch. 67[71] sts.
Work 2 rows.
Next row Patt to within last st, turn.
Rep the last row twice more. 64[68] sts.
188

Continue without shaping until leg measures 27½in from beg of crutch shaping or 2½in less than required length.
Next row 3ch to count as first htr, 1htr into next st, *(yrh, insert hook into next st and draw through loop, yrh and draw through 2 loops) 3 times into the same st, yrh and draw through all loops on hook—called bean st—, miss one st, rep from * to last 2 sts, 1htr into each st. 30[32] bean sts with 2htr at each end.
Next row 3ch to count as first htr, 1htr into next st, 1 bean st into each bean st, 1htr into each of last 2 sts.
Rep last row once more.
Next row 3ch to count as first htr, 1htr into next st, 2htr into each bean st, 1htr into each of last 2 sts. Fasten off.

Right leg

Work to match left Leg, reversing shaping.

Jacket back

Make 67[71]ch.
1st row 1htr into 3rd ch from hook, *miss 1ch, 1 bean st into next ch, rep from * to last 2 sts, 1htr into each of last 2 sts. 31[33] bean sts with 2htr at each end.
2nd row 3ch to count as first htr, 1htr into next st, 1 bean st into each bean st, 1htr into each of last 2 sts.
Rep the 2nd row until work measures 20in from beg or length required to armhole.

Shape armholes
Next row Ss over first 2htr and first bean st, 3ch, 1htr into next bean st, patt to within last 2 bean sts, 2htr into next bean st, turn.
Next row 3ch to count as first htr, 1htr into htr, 1htr into bean st, patt to within last bean st, 1htr into bean st, 1htr into each of last 2 sts.
Next row 3ch to count as first htr, yrh, insert hook into next st and draw through loop, insert hook into next st and draw through all 4 loops—

called dec 1—, patt to within last 3 sts, dec 1, 1htr into last st. 25[27] bean sts with 2htr at each end.
Continue without shaping until armholes measure 7[7½]in.

Shape shoulders
Next row Ss over 2htr and 3[4] bean sts, 3ch, 1htr into next bean st, 1 bean st into each of next 4 bean sts. Fasten off. Miss 9 bean sts in centre, rejoin yarn, 3ch, 1 bean st into each of next 4 bean sts, 2htr into next bean st. Fasten off.

Left front

Make 39[43]ch and work in patt as given for Back until work measures the same as Back to armholes. 17[19] bean sts.

Shape armhole
Next row Ss over 2htr and 1 bean st, 3ch, 1htr into next bean st, patt to end.
Next row Patt to within last bean st, 1htr into bean st, 1htr into each of last 2 sts.
Next row 3ch to count as first htr, dec 1, patt to end. 14[16] bean sts.
Continue without shaping until armhole measures 5in, ending at front edge.

Shape neck
Next row Ss over 2htr and 4[5] bean sts, 3ch, 1htr into next bean st, patt to end.
Next row Patt to within last bean st, 1htr into bean st, 1htr into each of last 2 sts.
Next row 3ch to count as first htr, dec 1, patt to end. 8[9] bean sts.
Continue without shaping until armhole measures the same as on Back, ending at armhole edge.

Shape shoulder
Next row Ss over htr and 3[4] bean sts, 3ch, 1htr into next bean st, patt to end.

Right front

Work to match left Front, reversing shaping.

Sleeves

Make 41[45]ch and work in patt as given for Back for 10 rows. 18[20] bean sts.
Next row 3ch to count as first htr, 2htr into the next st, patt to within last 2 sts, 2htr into next st, 1htr into last st.
Rep last row once more.
Next row 3ch to count as first htr, 1htr into next st, 1 bean st into next st, patt to end, ending with 2htr 20[22] bean sts.
Work 3 rows without shaping.
Rep the inc rows once more. 22[24] bean sts.
Continue without shaping until work measures 15in from beg.

Shape top
Next row Ss over 2htr and 1 bean st, 3ch, 1htr into next st, patt to within last 2 bean sts, 2htr into next bean st, turn.
Next row 3ch to count as first htr, 1htr into next st, 1htr into bean st, patt to within last bean st, 1htr into bean st, 1htr into each of last 2 sts.
Next row 3ch to count as first htr, dec 1, patt to within last 3 sts, dec 1, 1htr into last st. Rep last 2 rows 2[3] times more. Fasten off.

Collar

Join shoulder seams.
With WS facing, work 42[46] htr round neck edge.
Next row 2ch to count as first htr, 1htr into each st to end.
Next row 2ch to count as first htr, 1htr into each of next 3[5]htr, *2htr into next st, 1htr into each of next 2htr, rep from * 11 times more, 1htr into each of next 2[4]htr. 54[58] sts.
Continue in htr until collar measures 3in. Fasten off.

Belt

Make 8ch.
Next row 1htr into 3rd ch from hook, 1htr into each ch to end.

Continue in htr until work measures 30[32]in or required length.

Dec one st at each end of every row until 3 sts rem. Fasten off.

To make up

Press pieces under a dry cloth and using a cool iron.
Trousers. Join Back and Front seams. Join leg seams. Fold over first row at waist and slip stitch in place. Thread elastic through.
Jacket. Sew in sleeves. Join side and sleeve seams.
With RS facing, join yarn at lower corner of right Front and work 1 row of htr along front edge, round collar working 2htr into each corner, then down left front edge, turn.
Mark position of 8 buttonholes on right front edge placing bottom one 2in from lower edge, top one just below neck edge, then 6 more evenly spaced between.
Next row Work in htr to position of first buttonhole, (2ch, miss 2 sts, 1htr to next buttonhole) 7 times, 2ch, miss 2 sts, 1htr in each st to end.
Next row Work in htr with 2htr into each 2ch sp.
Work 1 more row in htr.
Fasten off.
Work 1 row htr round lower edge of jacket and sleeves.
Press all seams lightly. Sew on buttons. Sew buckle to straight end of belt.

A stylish suit in simple crochet ▶
▼ *Detail of bean stitch and treble*

Stitchery pattern/floral cushion

This charming floral design cushion would look attractive in either a traditional or a modern decor.

To make this cushion measuring 15 inches square you will need:

- ☐ Pieces of single weave canvas with 14 threads to 1 inch measuring 21 inches square
- ☐ Piece of fabric measuring 16 inches square for backing
- ☐ Zip fastener 10 inches long
- ☐ Crewel needle No.18
- ☐ Cushion pad measuring 16 inches square
- ☐ Appletons Crewel Wool in the amounts indicated in the following column.

The entire design is worked using diagonal tent stitch, worked over two threads of canvas, with three strands of crewel wool in the needle.

To make up

When the stitchery is complete, stretch and trim the canvas leaving ½ inch seam allowances. Make up into a cushion using a fabric backing. Leave a 10 inch opening on one side of the cushion and insert the zip fastener.

	Colour	No.	Skeins
1	Rose pink	759	1
2	Scarlet	505	1
3	Rose pink	755	1
4	Dull rose pink	144	1
5	Dull rose pink	142	3
6	Mauve	607	3
○	Mauve	604	1
╳	Mauve	602	1
·	Putty	981	2
⊟	Putty	983	2
∕	Putty	985	1
◁	Bright yellow	553	1
⊡	Lemon	996	1
∕	Chocolate	187	1
▲	Red brown	208	1
⋈	Honeysuckle yellow	697	1
●	Drab green	338	1
⋗	Drab green	335	2
△	Drab green	332	2
◉	Drab green	331	1
■	Bright peacock green	835	1
◹	Bright peacock green	832	1
╳	Bright peacock green	831	1
⊘	Peacock blue	641	1
☐	Background—off white	992	12

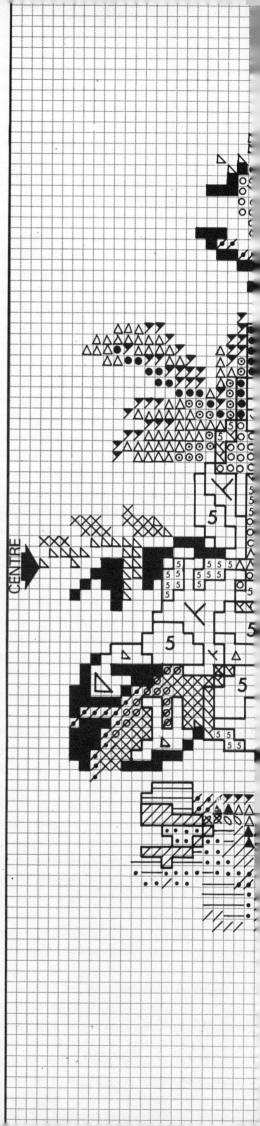

Stitchery design/mola work

San Blas appliqué

Bold, brilliant colours are used in this unique method of appliqué, worked by the Indian women of the San Blas Islands off the coast of Panama. The appliqué designs are now worked in two pieces measuring about 14 inches by 20 inches and are made into blouses called molas.

When the Indians first moved to the islands in about 1850 the molas were simple affairs, made only of dark blue material with a single band of red cloth around the bottom. The designs developed to decorate the lower half of the mola and then developed further to form a major part of the blouse. Later, when traders brought fabrics of brighter colours to the islands, the designs became more elabor-

192

ate, involving up to five or six layers of fabric in as many colours. Reds, oranges, greens and blues vibrated together in one design. The designs themselves are primitive and gay, representing forms and figures from everyday life on the islands. Gods, goddesses, shapes from nature such as animals and plants and important people are all featured in bold, primitive stylized shapes. Often the designs are copied from pictures in magazines, comic books, calendars and even labels on canned foods. The designs often include English words or letters which are not understood by the Spanish speaking Indians and used with complete disregard of their meaning, but which look decorative and important. The stylized designs of the molas reflect

the style of the wooden figures called 'nuchus', carved by the Sans Blas men. The layers of fabric are first tacked together and then cut away, and the result very much resembles the enamel work of some Mexicans, where layers of colour are applied (painted) then incised to reveal colour on colour.

The molas are an important status symbol amongst the Indians and in some places it is considered improper for a San Blas Indian girl to be married without possessing at least twelve or more unworn molas as part of her dowry.

Fabrics

For the traditional style San Blas appliqué, plain dyed fabrics such as poplin or

▲ *San Blas appliqué worked on the hem of a simple wrapover evening skirt*

sail cloth are ideal. However, pure silks or shantung would lend themselves beautifully to the technique. For the more ambitious, experiments with textured fabrics such as corduroy or tweed could prove interesting. Felt, suede or leather could also be used but no turnings would be needed.

Uses

This appliqué technique is ideal for fashion where rich, bold effects are required. It would look good worked as a border on a skirt, on an evening cloak, on inset panels or on a yoke on a dress or a blouse.

Mola work on curtains would look dramatic and cushion covers, bedspreads, pictures and wall hangings are all suitable subjects.

Method

This appliqué technique is more a method of cutting away than applying pieces of fabric. Parts of the top layers of fabric are cut away to reveal a section of the colour below. One, two or three layers of fabric may have to be cut through at the same time to get to the desired colour for a particular part of the design. However, if the colours are arranged well, it should not be necessary to have to cut through more than one layer of fabric at a time. Pieces of different colours can be placed under only certain parts of the design.

Experiment with two or three layers of fabric to start with, introducing extra colour by applying small areas of fabric to highlight the design.

Place the fabrics in the desired arrangement of colours then tack the layers of fabric together all round the edge and also diagonally across each way to hold them securely.

To reveal the first colour under the top layer, use a pair of sharp embroidery scissors and cut away a portion of the top fabric in the desired shape. Clip the edges of the fabric to be turned under on all curves and into all corners and turn in $\frac{1}{8}$ inch. Using a matching colour sewing thread, slip stitch the edge to the layer of fabric below. Small appliqués of another colour can be added in one, two or more layers using the same technique of cutting out to reveal the colour below.

193

Home crochet/lacy lampshade

This extremely simple pattern for a lampshade cover can either be used to fit in with a room scheme or to give new life to an old lampshade. Use the basic stitch pattern of straight and looped chain to make something else for your room to match up with the lampshade, such as a table mat, chair back cover or even curtains.

Size

To fit drum lampshade 11in deep by 10in top diameter by 10½in bottom diameter

---

Tension for this design
5 patts to 2¾in worked on No.3·00 hook

Materials shown here
Wendy Invitation Crochet Cotton, 5 25grm balls
One No.3·00 (ISR) crochet hook
One No.2·50 (ISR) crochet hook
One purchased drum lampshade 11in deep, 10in top diameter, 10½in bottom diameter

Main section

Using No.3·00 hook, make 192ch loosely. Join with ss to first ch.
1st round 7ch, 1dc into same ch as ss, 2ch, miss 2ch, 1dc into next ch, *7ch, 1dc into same ch, 2ch, miss 2ch, 1dc into next ch, rep from * to end, working last dc into ss at beg of round. 64 patts.
2nd round Ss to centre of first 7ch loop, *2ch, 1dc into next 7ch loop, rep from * to end, working last dc into centre of first ch loop.
3rd round *7ch, 1dc into same dc, 2ch, 1dc into next dc, rep from * to end, working last dc into last dc of previous round.
The 2nd and 3rd rounds form patt and are rep throughout.
Continue in patt until work measures about 5½in.
Change to No.2·50 hook and continue in patt until work measures 11in, ending with a 2nd round (1st patt round).

Top picot edging

Next round *4ch, 1dc into same dc into next sp, 1dc into next dc, rep from * to end. Fasten off.

Lower picot edging

Using No.2·50 hook, rejoin yarn to a ch into which dc have been worked.
Work 1dc, 4ch and 1dc into same ch, *1dc into each of the 2 missed ch between groups of dc of first round, 1dc into next ch, 4ch, 1dc into same ch, rep from * until 2ch remain, 1dc into each of next 2dc. Fasten off.

To make up

Press under a damp cloth, using a warm iron.
Place on lampshade and catch stitch in place round edges.

▼ *Several ideas around the home to make from the basic stitch pattern*

Cover to brighten a lampshade, new or old ►

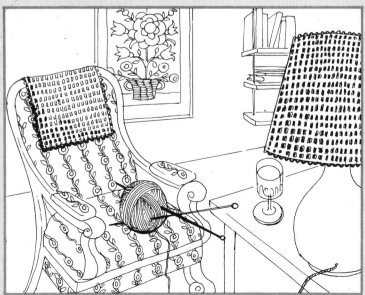

Tailoring four

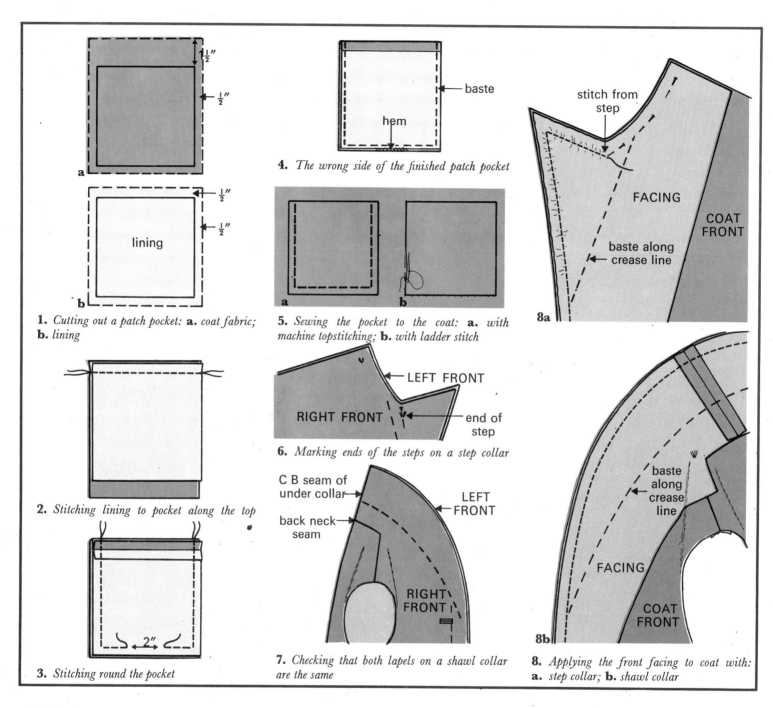

1. *Cutting out a patch pocket:* **a.** *coat fabric;* **b.** *lining*

2. *Stitching lining to pocket along the top*

3. *Stitching round the pocket*

4. *The wrong side of the finished patch pocket*

5. *Sewing the pocket to the coat:* **a.** *with machine topstitching;* **b.** *with ladder stitch*

6. *Marking ends of the steps on a step collar*

7. *Checking that both lapels on a shawl collar are the same*

8. *Applying the front facing to coat with:* **a.** *step collar;* **b.** *shawl collar*

In this chapter
A. Patch pockets
B. Facing the coat front: coat with lapels; coat without lapels.
C. Belts: belt across back; $\frac{1}{4}$ belt at side seams; $\frac{1}{2}$ belt at back; tie belt; belt with buckle.
D. The second fitting: preparing for the fitting; the fitting stages; set in sleeve; raglan sleeve.
*Terms and stitches

A. Patch pockets

1a, b. Cut out pocket shape with $\frac{1}{2}$ inch seam allowance all round plus an extra 1 inch along top edge (**a**). Then cut out lining 1 inch shorter than the pocket (**b**).
196

2. Stitch lining to pocket along the top, taking $\frac{1}{2}$ inch seam.   Press seam open.
3. Fold lining to pocket as shown, right sides facing. Stitch, leaving a 2 inch opening at the lower edge. Snip curved seams if any or snip across corners.
4. Turn through the opening, baste flat round edges and hem opening to close. Press and clap.
5. Apply to coat by topstitching (**a**) or ladder stitch* (**b**).

B. Facing the coat front

Coat with lapels
6. If working on a step collar mark the steps on the top edges of the lapels so they are both the same.

7. If working on a shawl collar, stitch and press the centre back seam of the under collar, then stitch the shoulder and back neck seams. Press open and clap. Fold the coat in half and check that both sides have the same curve.
8a, b. Lay the facing and coat right sides together. Baste with small stitches to control the slight fullness there may be on the facing of the lapels.
Baste along crease line.
Stitch carefully as given on the instruction sheet, taking care to keep both lapels the same. Note that the step collar is only stitched as far as the end of the step.

Vogue 2573 has welt pockets and a tie belt
Butterick pattern 6528 has raglan sleeves ▶

9a, b. Remove basting. Snip across corners, snip into the end of the stitching line if applicable, and layer the seam allowances.

Press the seam open over a pressing roll.

10a, b. Turn facing to the inside. Working on the underside of the lapel baste the seam edge of the lapel so that it lies away from the top edge and baste along the crease line. Baste the remainder of the facing seam to lie away from the top of the coat.

To press the lapel lay it flat, right side down, on an ironing board. Cover with a damp cloth and press as far as the crease line. Clap.

Press and clap the rest of the front edge. Lay the coat right side up with lapel folded in position and lightly press over a ham, using a woollen cloth under the pressing cloth.

Press the wrong side of the lower coat on a flat board.

11. Side stitch* under the lapel and down the inside front to keep the seam in position.

Coat without lapels

Apply the facing as given on your pattern instruction sheet and follow the steps given above for coats with lapels, ignoring those points referring specifically to the lapels.

12. So the whole of the front seam edge should be basted to lie towards the inside of the coat and then side stitched* as shown.

C. Belts

You can add your own belt to a plain coat to give back interest.

13a—e. The belt can be set into the side seams and go right across the back (**a**). It can be set into the side seams and sewn or buttoned at the side back (**b**). It can be set across the centre back (**c**). You can have a tie belt (**d**) or a buckled belt (**e**).

14. For all belts you will need two pieces of the coat fabric each to the required width plus ½ inch seam allowance all round and one piece of interfacing to the same measurements.

15. If you are making buttonholes, baste the interfacing to the wrong side of one belt piece and make the buttonhole, as shown.

16. Place the belt pieces together, right sides facing, and lay the interfacing on the top. Baste together.

Belt across back

17. Stitch the long edges, layer the seam allowances, turn, baste and press.

18. Topstitch to match coat if required.

198

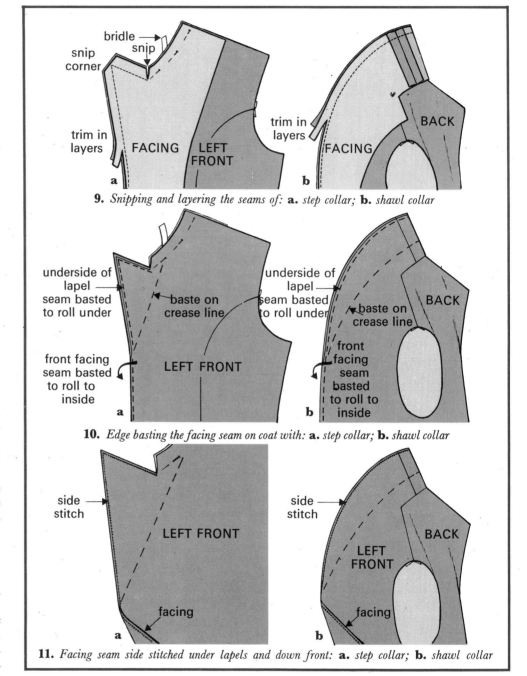

9. *Snipping and layering the seams of:* **a.** *step collar;* **b.** *shawl collar*

10. *Edge basting the facing seam on coat with:* **a.** *step collar;* **b.** *shawl collar*

11. *Facing seam side stitched under lapels and down front:* **a.** *step collar;* **b.** *shawl collar*

19a, b. When fitting make sure the belt is correctly balanced for the figure, usually above the waist for a short figure (**a**) and below the waist for a tall figure (**b**).

Quarter belt at side seams

20. Make buttonholes and shape the end.

21. Stitch long edges and across shaped end.

Snip and layer the seam allowances, turn, baste and press.

Topstitch if required.

22a, b. When fitting make sure that both belts are balanced and the same length. The belt should be just above the waist for a short figure (**a**) and just below the waist for a tall figure (**b**).

Half belt at back

23. Make buttonholes and shape ends.

24. Stitch the belt all round leaving a 2 to 4 inch opening along one side.

Snip and layer the seam allowances, turn, baste and press. Hem opening to close.

Topstitch if required.

When fitting check for balance as for the belt across the back (figure **19**).

Tie belt

25. Make up as for ½ belt at back.

Belt with buckle

Make up as for ¼ belt.

26. Fold unstitched end through buckle. Turn under raw ends and herringbone.

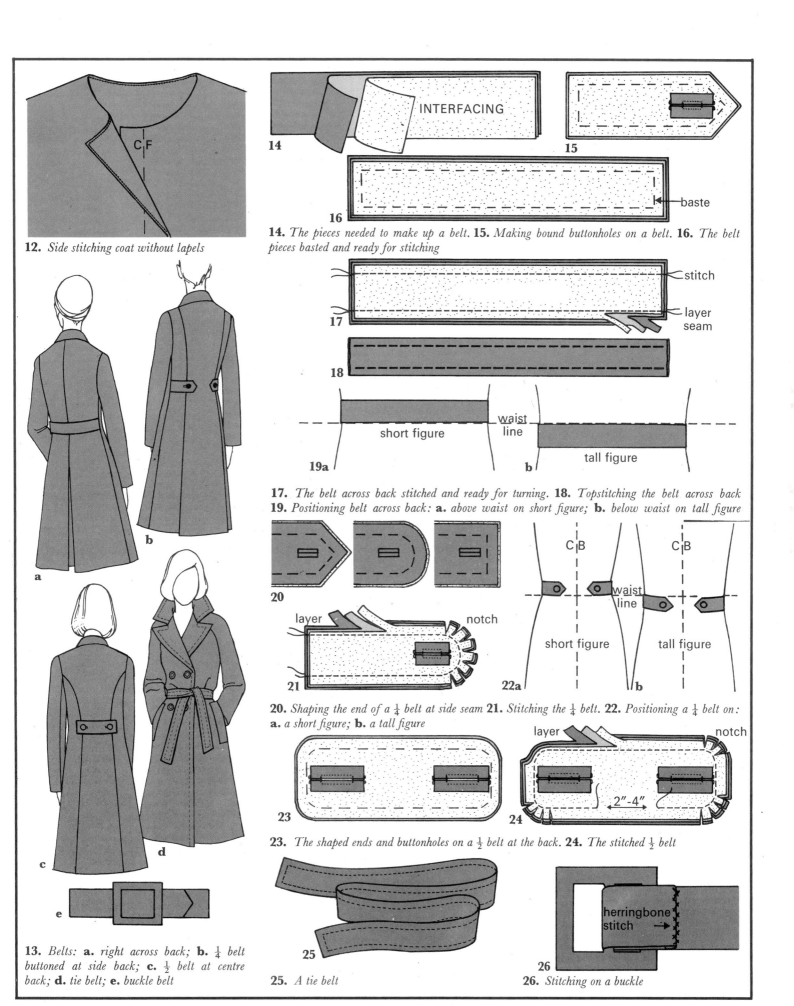

12. *Side stitching coat without lapels*

INTERFACING

baste

14. *The pieces needed to make up a belt.* **15.** *Making bound buttonholes on a belt.* **16.** *The belt pieces basted and ready for stitching*

stitch

layer seam

waist line

short figure

tall figure

17. *The belt across back stitched and ready for turning.* **18.** *Topstitching the belt across back*
19. *Positioning belt across back:* **a.** *above waist on short figure;* **b.** *below waist on tall figure*

layer

notch

C B

C B

waist line

short figure

tall figure

20. *Shaping the end of a ¼ belt at side seam* **21.** *Stitching the ¼ belt.* **22.** *Positioning a ¼ belt on:*
a. *a short figure;* **b.** *a tall figure*

layer

notch

2"-4"

23. *The shaped ends and buttonholes on a ½ belt at the back.* **24.** *The stitched ½ belt*

13. *Belts:* **a.** *right across back;* **b.** *¼ belt buttoned at side back;* **c.** *½ belt at centre back;* **d.** *tie belt;* **e.** *buckle belt*

25. *A tie belt*

herringbone stitch

26. *Stitching on a buckle*

199

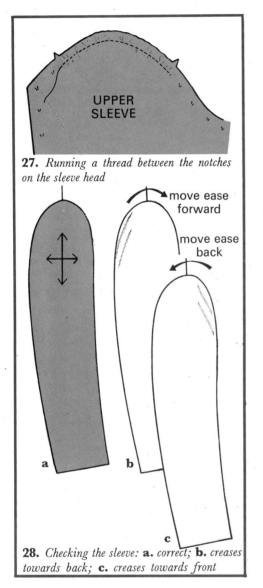

27. *Running a thread between the notches on the sleeve head*

28. *Checking the sleeve:* **a.** *correct;* **b.** *creases towards back;* **c.** *creases towards front*

▲ *Close-up of a raglan sleeve set in position. From Butterick pattern 6528*

D. The second fitting

Having made the coat fronts, belt (if required) and stitched the back seams, it is now time for the second fitting.

Preparing for the fitting
Working on the new fitting lines, baste the side seams. Baste the shoulder seams if not already sewn. Over baste the under collar (Tailoring 2, A).
27. Sew a running thread between the notches on the sleeve heads to help distribute the ease and baste the sleeves into the armholes.
Add shoulder pads if required.

The fitting stages
☐ Check all the points made in Tailoring 2.
☐ Turn up the hem. If the coat has a tie or buckled belt, put on the belt before adjusting the hem as the length will be affected.
☐ Other belts are positioned after the

hem has been turned up. The coat must not be cut in half by a belt, it should give a balanced, pleasing look.
☐ Check the length again with the belt in position.
☐ Check that the sleeve is not too tight or too loose.
☐ Turn up the sleeve hem.

Set in sleeve
28a. Take a good look at each sleeve head. The grain should be square and there should be no creases.
28b. If there are creases towards the back, unbaste and move the ease slightly towards the front. If this is not enough then unbaste the complete sleeve and move it forwards.
28c. If there are creases towards the front then reverse the process moving the ease to the back.

Raglan sleeve
Check that the sleeves are not too full at the shoulders. Any fullness should be

pinned into the dart or seam which runs down the shoulder into the arm.

*Terms and stitches

Ladder stitch (29): used for invisibly stitching a pocket to a garment.

Side stitch (30): used for flattening edges of lapels and collars. Make a tiny stitch at right angles to the line of stitching. The stitches should not appear on the right side of the garment.

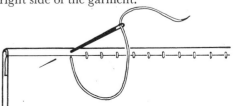